USING THE MOUSE AND SCROLL BAR TO MOVE THE DOCUMENT VIEW

TO MOVE DOCUMENT VIEW...	DO THIS...
Up 5 lines	Click the up arrow at the top of the scroll bar
Down 5 lines	Click the down arrow at the bottom of the scroll bar
Up one page	Click between the scroll button and the up arrow
Down one page	Click between the scroll button and the down arrow
To the beginning of the document	Drag the scroll button to the top of the scroll bar
To the end of the document	Drag the scroll button to the bottom of the scroll bar
Anywhere in the document	Drag the scroll button to the desired position

SYBEX **LEARN FAST!** BOOKS

The SYBEX *Learn Fast!* series offers busy, computer-literate people two books in one: a quick, hands-on tutorial guide to program essentials, and a comprehensive reference to commands and features.

The first half of each *Learn Fast!* book teaches the basic operations and underlying concepts of the topic software. These lessons feature trademark SYBEX characteristics: step-by-step procedures; thoughtful, well-chosen examples; an engaging writing style; valuable margin notes; and plenty of practical insights.

Once you've learned the basics, you're ready to start working on your own. That's where the second half of each *Learn Fast!* book comes in. This alphabetical reference offers concise instructions for using program commands, dialog boxes, and menu options. With dictionary-style organization and headings, this half of the book is designed to give you fast access to information.

SYBEX is very interested in your reactions to the *Learn Fast!* series. Your opinions and suggestions will help all of our readers, including yourself. Please send your comments to: SYBEX Editorial Department, 2021 Challenger Dr. Alameda, CA 94501.

LEARN *WordPerfect for Windows* FAST!

my version is 5.1

LEARN *WordPerfect® for Windows*™ FAST!

PETER G. AITKEN

SYBEX®

San Francisco . Paris . Düsseldorf . Soest

Acquisitions Editor: David Clark
Series Editor: James A. Compton
Editor: Kathleen Lattinville
Technical Editor: Rebecca M. Lyles
Word Processors: Ann Dunn, Susan Trybull
Book Designer: Claudia Smelser
Chapter Art and Paste-Up: Charlotte Carter
Screen Graphics: Cuong Le
Desktop Publishing Production: Len Gilbert
Proofreader/Production Assistant: Janet K. Boone
Indexer: Nancy Guenther
Cover Designer: Ingalls + Associates
Cover Photographer: Michael Lamotte
Screen reproductions produced with Collage Plus.
Collage Plus is a trademark of Inner Media Inc.

Library of Congress Card Number: 92-80315
ISBN: 0-7821-1100-9

Manufactured in the United States of America
10 9 8 7 6 5 4 3 2 1

ACKNOWLEDGMENTS

This book owes a great deal to the following people: Jim Compton, series editor; Kathleen Lattinville, editor; and Rebecca Lyles, technical editor.

TABLE*of*CONTENTS

(handwritten note) actual model Panasonic KX-P2123

(handwritten note) Printer installed as Default printer Panasonic KX-P2123 on LPT1: WP6 Default print

(handwritten note) Nap printer HP LaserJet 4/4M on LPT 1:

PREFACE

Welcome to *Learn WordPerfect for Windows Fast!* This book offers a unique approach to learning this powerful word processing program. The combination of a tutorial with a reference section provides material that would normally require you to purchase—and read!—two books. You save both time and money.

The tutorial section uses hands-on lessons with step-by-step instructions to teach you the fundamentals of WordPerfect for Windows. You will "learn by doing" as you create, edit, and print practice documents:

- Lessons 1 and 2 teach you the basics of creating, editing, and saving a document.

- Lessons 3 through 5 show you how to enhance your document's appearance by controlling formatting, fonts, and page layout.

- Lesson 6 shows you how to print your document.

- Lesson 7 teaches you how to use macros to speed up your work.

- Lesson 8 explains how to set program preferences, check spelling, add document comments, and apply several other useful techniques.

- Lesson 9 shows you how to work with multiple documents at one time.

I suggest that you work through all of the lessons, in order. When you're finished, you'll have the skills needed to start using WordPerfect for Windows for real-world tasks.

The second part of this book is an alphabetical reference of WordPerfect for Windows features. You can refer to this section as you work though the tutorial, and afterwards as you continue to work with the program. Reference entries are arranged alphabetically by task, with cross references where needed.

The reference section covers many more program features than are included in the tutorial. It does not, however, cover each and every feature of WordPerfect for Windows. To do so would require a book much larger than this one! I have tried to include the most frequently needed operations, and omit only the most specialized ones.

PART ONE

Tutorial

LESSON 1

GETTING STARTED

INTRODUCING

The WordPerfect for Windows screen

Pull-down menus, dialog boxes, and the Button Bar

Entering text

This first lesson starts you on your way to becoming a proficient WordPerfect for Windows user. You'll learn how to start WordPerfect for Windows, use the menus and dialog boxes, and enter commands. You'll also create your first document and save it to disk. Let's get started!

STARTING WORDPERFECT FOR WINDOWS

Before you can use WordPerfect for Windows, you must install it on your system. If you have not installed it yet, do so now, following the instructions in the Appendix.

Start Windows and you will see the Program Manager screen, shown in Figure 1.1. If Windows is already running and the Program Manager screen is not visible, press Alt+Esc one or more times until it is displayed.

FIGURE 1.1:

The Program
Manager screen

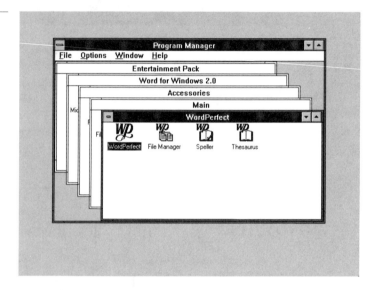

The Program Manager screen has windows for the programs you have installed, one of which will be titled WordPerfect. The WordPerfect window contains several icons that represent the different components of WordPerfect for Windows. To start the program, select the icon labeled WordPerfect. Either double-click the icon with the mouse, or highlight it with the ← and → keys and press ↵.

If the WordPerfect window is not on top of the Program Manager screen (as it is in Figure 1.1), press Ctrl+F6 one or more times until it is.

WordPerfect will display its logo for a few seconds, and then you will see the program main screen, shown in Figure 1.2. You need to learn the components of this screen to use the program effectively.

GETTING TO KNOW THE WORDPERFECT FOR WINDOWS SCREEN

Figure 1.2 shows the most important parts of the WordPerfect for Windows screen.

- The *title bar* displays the name of the program and the name of the document being edited.

- The *menu bar* displays the main program commands. When you select a command from the menu bar, its pull-down menu with additional commands is displayed.

- The *work area* is where you enter and edit text.

- The *insertion point* is a small blinking vertical line that marks the location where text you type will appear.

- The *scroll bar* is used to scroll through a document with the mouse.

- The *status bar* displays information about the document. At the right end of the status line you see the current position of the insertion point: page number (Pg), vertical inches from top of the page (Ln), and horizontal inches from the left edge of the page (Pos). The left end of the status bar displays various types of information depending on what you're doing. The default display is the current font.

FIGURE 1.2:

The WordPerfect for Windows opening screen

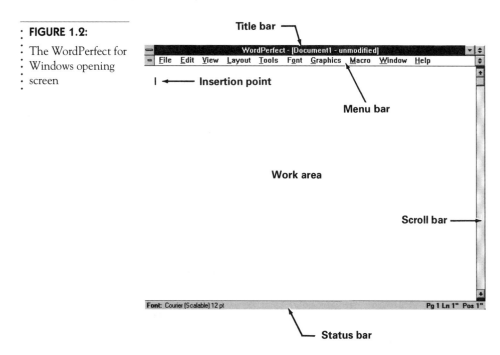

USING THE MENU SYSTEM

The screen elements you've just looked at should be familiar if you've worked with other Windows programs. Every program designed for Windows communicates in essentially the same way, using a common set of components and conventions defined by Microsoft. If you already know how to use another Windows program, you may want to skip ahead to the section "Creating Your First Document." If not, you should first become familiar with the following concepts and techniques.

THE MENU BAR

The menu bar gives you access to all of Wordperfect's features. Selecting any of its commands leads to a pull-down menu of further commands, such as the Edit menu illustrated in Figure 1.3.

You can select an item from the menu bar using either the mouse or the keyboard. With the mouse, click on the desired command. With the keyboard, you can either press Alt plus the underlined letter (for example, Alt+E for the Edit menu), or press F10 to activate the menu and use the arrow keys and ↵ to select a command.

PULL-DOWN MENUS

In the pull-down menu in Figure 1.3, you see several special conventions:

- A key or key combination listed next to a pull-down menu command is a *shortcut key*. You can select the command directly with this key or key

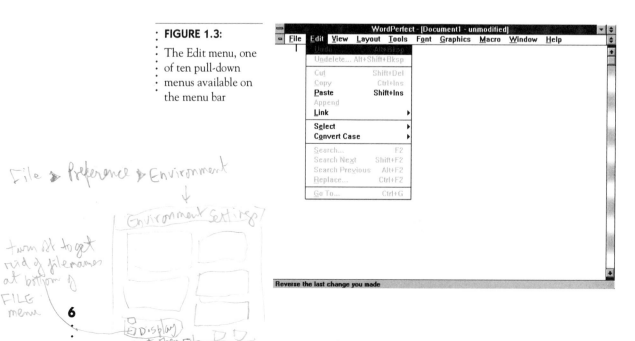

FIGURE 1.3:

The Edit menu, one of ten pull-down menus available on the menu bar combination without using the menu bar. For example, you can select the Search command by pressing F2. Shortcut keys are provided for only the most commonly needed pull-down menu commands.

♦ An ellipsis (...) following a pull-down menu command indicates that selecting the command leads to a dialog box (for example, the Search command in Figure 1.3). Dialog boxes are explained later in this lesson.

♦ An arrowhead next to a pull-down menu command means that the command leads to another submenu, called a *cascade* menu (for example, the Select command in Figure 1.3).

♦ A checkmark next to a menu item indicates that the item is currently "on." Selecting the item will turn it off (or, if it is already off, will turn it on).

♦ A command displayed in grayed text (for example, the Cut command in Figure 1.3) is not available at the present time.

You'll save time if you learn the shortcut keys for commands you use frequently.

Once you have displayed a pull-down menu, you have several options for selecting one of the commands:

♦ Click the desired command with the mouse.

♦ Use the ↑ and ↓ keys to highlight the desired command, and then press ↵.

♦ Press the key corresponding to the underlined letter in the desired command.

Note that when the menu system is active, the status bar at the bottom of the screen displays a brief description of the highlighted menu command (for example, the Undo command in Figure 1.3).

If you make a mistake entering menu commands, either press the Esc key one or more times to "back out" of the menus, or use the mouse to click anywhere outside of the menus.

USING DIALOG BOXES

WordPerfect for Windows displays a dialog box whenever it needs more information from you to carry out a command. All WordPerfect for Windows dialog boxes follow the same basic principles. If you learn a few simple procedures, you'll be able to use all dialog boxes.

Each dialog box has a title at the top that identifies the box's function. Inside the dialog box are one or more of the following elements (labeled in Figures 1.4 and 1.5):

- A *text box* is used to enter text or numbers. Some text boxes start out blank, and you must fill them in. Others start with a default entry, which you can either accept or modify. Click in the box or tab to it, and start typing at the insertion point.

- A *list box* displays a list of items from which you can choose. In most cases a list box is coupled with a text box—the item you select in the list box is automatically copied to the text box. Click a list item to select it.

- A *checkbox* is used for options that are not mutually exclusive. You can have none, one, or many checkbox options selected at a time. Click on a box to turn it on or off.

- A *pop-up list* is similar to a list box except that only the currently selected item is displayed. To make a different selection, you must open the pop-up list by pointing on the arrow and pressing the left mouse button. Then drag to the desired item and release the button.

- *Command buttons* are used to accept or cancel the dialog box entries. One command button, usually labeled OK, executes the command using the information in the dialog box. Click this button only when you are satisfied with all of the dialog box entries. Another button, usually labeled Cancel or Close, closes the dialog box without executing the command. Some dialog boxes contain command buttons that perform other tasks.

- *Radio buttons*, also called option buttons, are used to select from a group of mutually exclusive options. Only one option at a time can be selected, indicated by a filled-in circle.

When a dialog box is displayed, only one component in the box is selected, or active, at any one time. The selected item is outlined by a dashed box, or, for a text box, its contents are highlighted. In Figure 1.5, for example, the Number of Columns box is selected.

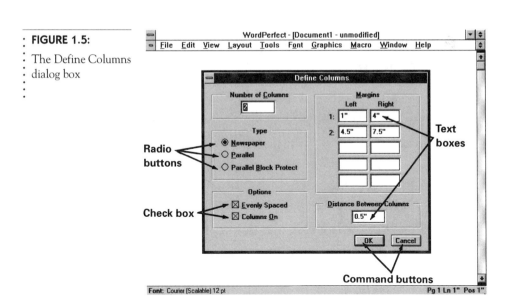

FIGURE 1.4:

The Save As dialog box

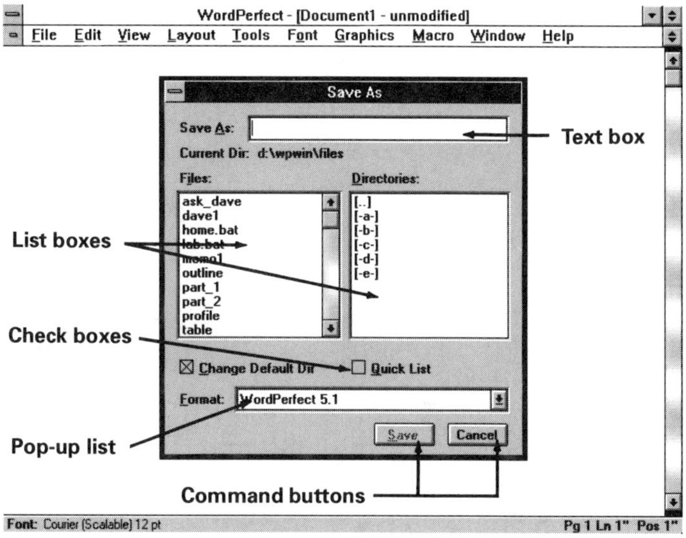

FIGURE 1.5:

The Define Columns dialog box

Using the Keyboard

If you're a touch-typist, or if a mouse is not available, you can use the following keyboard techniques in a dialog box:

- ◆ To make a dialog box item active, press Tab and Shift+Tab to move forward and backward between items. Or, press Alt plus the underlined letter in the item's name.

- To select an item in a list box, first make the list box active, and then use the ↓ and ↑ keys to highlight the desired item.

- To toggle a radio button or checkbox on or off, select the item, and then press the spacebar.

- To select an item in a pop-up box, first select the box. Then press the spacebar to open it, and use the ↑ and ↓ keys to highlight the desired item in the list.

WARNING

When a dialog box is displayed, do not press ↵ unless you want the selected command executed.

Editing a Text Box

After you select a text box, you can enter new information or edit the default information that is already displayed there. When a text box is first made active, its contents are highlighted. If you press any regular typing key (for example, a letter or number), the highlighted text is erased and replaced by what you type. To edit the contents of the text box, press any arrow key to remove the highlight. The *insertion point,* where editing actions will occur, is marked by a vertical line. You can edit the text in the box as follows:

- Type in as many new characters as desired. If you reach the right edge of the box, the contents will scroll to the left to make room for new text.

- Use the → and ← keys to move the insertion point one character at a time. Or, click on the new position.

- Use the Home and End keys to move the insertion point to the beginning or end of the box.

- Highlight one or more characters by pressing and holding Shift, and then pressing → or ←.

- Press Del to delete either the highlighted characters or one character to the right of the insertion point.

- Press Backspace to delete the character to the left of the insertion point.

After entering the desired text in a text box, *do not* press ↵ unless you are ready to close the dialog box and execute the command.

CLOSING A DIALOG BOX

When you have made all necessary entries in the dialog box and are ready to execute the command, click the OK (or Start or Accept) command button or press ⏎. If you change your mind, close the dialog box without executing the command by clicking the Cancel (or Close or Abort) button, or by pressing Esc.

THE BUTTON BAR

WordPerfect for Windows has a nifty tool called the *Button Bar* that simplifies access to several of the most frequently needed commands. When the Button Bar is displayed, you can select these commands by simply clicking on the proper button—you do not have to use the menu system.

The Button Bar is displayed immediately below the menu bar, as shown in Figure 1.6. You have the option of displaying the Button Bar or keeping it hidden. To display the Button Bar (or hide it if it is already displayed), select View from the menu bar and then select Button Bar from the pull-down menu.

Now that you know how to select menu commands, I will use a shorthand method of showing command sequences. For example, rather than saying "select View from the menu bar, and then select Button Bar from the pull-down menu," I'll simply say "select View ➤ Button Bar."

You'll learn about all the commands on the Button Bar over the course of the tutorial.

FIGURE 1.6:

The Button Bar offers mouse shortcuts for frequently needed commands

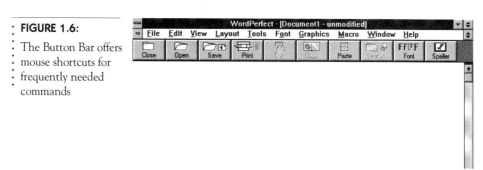

CREATING YOUR FIRST DOCUMENT

You've now learned enough of the basics of WordPerfect for Windows to create your first document. This short, simple document, shown in Figure 1.7, will give you a feel for working in WordPerfect for Windows.

ENTERING TEXT

To enter the text of the memo, simply begin typing it in at your keyboard, starting with the date. You'll see that each character you type appears on the screen, and the insertion point moves to the right. Once you've entered the date, press ↵ twice: once to end the date line, a second time to create a blank line. Continue, entering the To:, From:, and Re: lines in the same manner, pressing ↵ twice at the end of each line.

Please see the Date entry in Part II.

When you type in the main text of the memo, you may notice a couple of spelling mistakes in the example. *They are intentional!* Just type them in as you see them and we will correct them later.

FIGURE 1.7:

A one-page memo

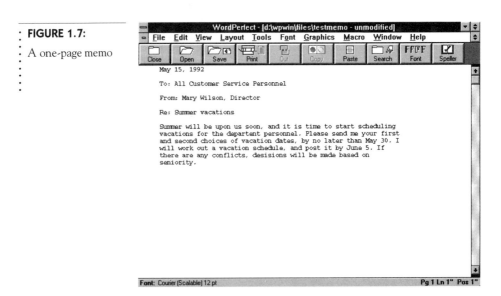

CORRECTING MISTAKES

Unless you are a perfect typist, most documents you create will contain a few errors. Let's fix the intentional mistakes in the memo you just typed. Look over the document on your screen to locate the mistakes. To correct them, you must first move the insertion point to the mistake. With the mouse, move the pointer to the desired location and click. (Note that the mouse pointer changes from an arrow to a vertical I-beam when it is in the text area.) With the keyboard, use the ← → ↑ and ↓ keys to move the insertion point one character or line at a time in the indicated direction. Now, let's correct the mistakes:

1. Move the insertion point in front of the second *e* in "departent," and then type in an **m**.

2. Move the insertion point in front of the first *s* in "desisions." Press Del to delete the *s*, and then type in a **c**.

It's as simple as that! If you made any other mistakes in typing the memo, use these techniques to correct them. In Lesson 2 you'll learn more about adding, deleting, and editing text.

SAVING THE DOCUMENT

The memo that you just entered is stored in your computer's memory, but it will be erased when you turn the computer off. To have it available for future use, you must save it on disk. The first time that you save a document you need to assign it a name. Let's call this practice memo TESTMEMO. To save TESTMEMO, follow these steps:

1. Select File ➤ Save. The Save As dialog box is displayed, as shown in Figure 1.4.

2. Enter the document name TESTMEMO in the Save As text box.

3. Click the Save command button or press ↵ to save the document.

After you save the document, notice that the title bar displays the name you assigned to the document. You can now continue working on the document if you want further practice entering and editing text. Or, if you're finished, you can exit WordPerfect for Windows. That's what we'll do next.

For filenames, WordPerfect for Windows follows the rules established by DOS: up to eight characters (letters, numbers, and the underscore character), optionally followed by a period and a one- to three-character extension.

EXITING WORDPERFECT FOR WINDOWS

When you're finished working in WordPerfect for Windows, you must exit the program. To do so, select File ➤ Exit or press the shortcut key Alt+F4. The program terminates, and you are returned to the Windows Program Manager screen. If a document has not yet been saved to disk, you'll see a dialog box asking whether to save it before exiting.

SUMMARY

This first lesson has started you on your way to becoming a proficient WordPerfect for Windows user. You've learned how to start the program, enter commands, and use dialog boxes. You also created and saved your first document. This introduction should have given you a feel for the power and ease-of-use of WordPerfect for Windows.

FOR MORE INFORMATION

You will find additional information about the topics covered in this lesson by consulting these reference entries in Part II:

Button Bar

Saving a Document

LESSON 2

CREATING AND EDITING A DOCUMENT

INTRODUCING

Opening a document on disk
Entering and editing text
Searching for text

When you use a word processing program such as WordPerfect for Windows, most of your time will be spent entering and editing text. This lesson teaches you the fundamentals of working with a document. For editing practice you'll use the memo that you created and saved in the last lesson. Before you can edit it, you must open it.

OPENING A DOCUMENT

When you start WordPerfect for Windows you are presented with a blank screen. From here you can start a new document, as you have learned earlier. In many instances, however, you will want to open a previously saved document and continue working on it. To open a document, follow these steps:

1. Select File ➤ Open, press F4, or click the Open button on the Button Bar. The Open File dialog box is displayed (Figure 2.1).

2. If you know the name of the file, type it into the Filename text box. Otherwise, select the desired file from the Files list box. For this example you should type in or select TESTMEMO.

3. Press ↵ or select Open. The specified document is displayed on the screen, ready for editing.

See the Retrieving a File entry in Part II.

FIGURE 2.1:
The Open File
dialog box

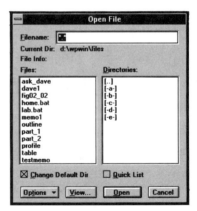

MOVING AROUND THE DOCUMENT

You move the insertion point to control where text is entered and edited. You learned the basics of moving the insertion point in the last lesson, when you made corrections in the sample memo. WordPerfect for Windows provides a number of keystroke shortcuts for moving the insertion point. In addition, you can scroll the document, bringing different parts of the document into view on the screen.

Call-E Lab opens Windows

The Call-E Computing Laboratory in the Faculty of Engineering Science recently filled a gap in both its computing hardware and its teaching capability with 15 new Microsoft Windows-equipped computers.

The computers will be used this fall for a second year Engineering Science computer course that will give students an overview of computing and applications.

A $20,000 contribution by the Undergraduate Engineering Society to the new network was matched by the Dean of Engineering Science. The funds were used for the purchase of the 15 computers in the network as well as software licenses.

Course instructor Prof. Ralph Buchal, Faculty of Engineering Science, said the course will not "teach specific software packages." Rather, it will introduce students to what software tools are out there for different kinds of tasks in the office and the lab.

The objective is to get students comfortable with using a computer as an everyday tool. Said Buchal: "If you find a computer hard to use, it's not because you're stupid, it's because the software is hard to learn."

The computers are Mustang brand PCs purchased at Western's Campus Computer Store. Each computer is equipped with an Intel 80486 processor, Microsoft Windows, 16 Megabytes of memory, a 215 Megabyte hard disk drive and a video accelerator card. *[handwritten: @ 2,666]*

Through the network, users of the computer can run top Windows software including Microsoft Word (word processor), Microsoft Excel (spreadsheet), and MathCAD (a powerful mathematics design program).

Why Microsoft Windows applications?

"Windows has seen the most software development of any operating system in recent years."

other computers such as the Apple Macintosh or a UNIX computer running one of that operating system's many graphical interfaces.

The Call-E lab is more a collection of computer network sites than one lab. The visitor discovers decidedly different things going on in different rooms.

In one room, there is a network of six-year-old IBM PS/2 computers used to teach first year students programming. Down the hall and around the corner, there is a room filled with powerful UNIX-based Silicon Graphics workstations used for high-end computer-aided design (CAD).

Between the low-end PS/2s and the high-end UNIX workstations is a room containing the network of new 486 PCs. There is also a room across the hall with a network of less powerful 386 computers.

Microcomputer hardware has grown a great deal in power while dropping sharply in price in recent years. The PS/2 machines, based on Intel 80286 processors, were considered cutting edge when installed five years ago. They are now considered not suitable for the requirements of the new Windows network.

"We've had two or three evolutions in computer hardware since those PS/2s were installed," said Call-E Manager of Computer Services Barry Kay.

The new computers have been built with an eye on future evolution in the computer hardware and software. They will be able to run Microsoft's new Windows NT operating system and they are upgradable to Intel's new faster Pentium microprocessor.

While it looks and feels a lot like Windows, NT is a completely new operating system that can better use the lab's 486 computer hardware capabilities. It also has better network capabilities.

"We bought the machines with an eye to expansion," said Kay.

Mustang star turns Cowboy

Former Mustang star Tyrone Williams has made the 47-man roster of the Dallas Cowboys in the National Football League. Williams will be one of six wide receivers on the Cowboys and has a $250,000 contract with the team. It is expected that the Cowboys will use Williams largely on specialty teams this season. Williams spent the 1992 season on the Cowboys' practice roster.

WESTERN'S FOUNDING 1863

Huron College

COMPUTER LAB

WordPerfect SIX.O

aid Call-E Laboratory program-
er Allan Zander.

Windows is not the only raphical User Interface (called UI) for a computer system, said ander. But it is the one that has rown most in popularity.

Buchal added that similarities etween GUIs are such that general principles learned on a Windows machine can be applied to

Enthusiastic Frosh

KEYSTROKE SHORTCUTS

Table 2.1 below lists the keystrokes that you can use to move the insertion point. Note that if you move the insertion point to an off-screen location, WordPerfect for Windows automatically scrolls to bring that portion of the document into view. Also, if you hold any key down, it automatically repeats; you can use this feature to move long distances. Take a few minutes now to practice moving the insertion point in your sample memo.

TABLE 2.1: Keystrokes for Moving the Insertion Point

KEYSTROKE	MOVEMENT
← or →	Left or right one character
↑ or ↓	Up or down one line
Ctrl+←	To the beginning of the previous word
Ctrl+→	To the beginning of the next word
Ctrl+↑	To the beginning of the previous paragraph
Ctrl+↓	To the beginning of the next paragraph
Home	To the beginning of the line
End	To the end of the line
PgUp	Up one screen
PgDn	Down one screen
Alt+Home	To the top of the current page
Alt+End	To the end of the current page
Ctrl+Home	To the start of the document
Ctrl+End	To the end of the document
Alt+PgUp	To the previous page
Alt+PgDn	To the next page

SCROLLING WITH THE MOUSE

You can use the mouse and the *scroll bar* to move around your document. The scroll bar is displayed along the right edge of your screen. Its parts are labeled in Figure 2.2.

The location of the scroll button on the scroll bar indicates the relative position of the current screen view to the entire document. For example, if the button is near the top of the scroll bar, the screen shows text near the beginning of the document.

FIGURE 2.2:

The components of the scroll bar

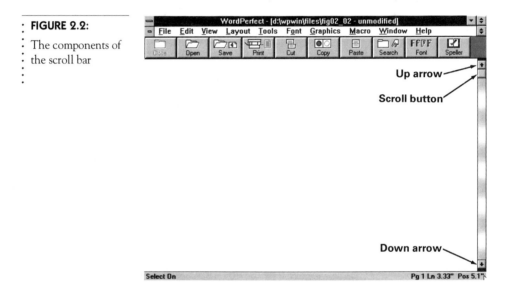

Table 2.2 lists scrolling movements you can make with the mouse and the scroll bar. This table introduces a new mouse action, *dragging*, which means positioning the mouse pointer at one location, pressing and holding the left mouse button, moving the pointer to another location, and then releasing the button.

When you scroll with the mouse, the insertion point does not move. After scrolling with the mouse, you have two choices:

- To move the insertion point to the location you just scrolled to, click with the mouse or press any arrow key.

- To scroll back to the original insertion-point location, type any character (letter, number, or spacebar).

TABLE 2.2: Using the Mouse and Scroll Bar to Move the Document View

TO MOVE YOUR VIEW OF THE DOCUMENT...	DO THIS...
Up 5 lines	Click the up arrow at the top of the scroll bar
Down 5 lines	Click the down arrow at the bottom of the scroll bar
Up one page	Click between the scroll button and the up arrow
Down one page	Click between the scroll button and the down arrow
To the beginning of the document	Drag the scroll button to the top of the scroll bar
To the end of the document	Drag the scroll button to the bottom of the scroll bar
Anywhere in the document	Drag the scroll button to the desired position

The ability to scroll without moving the insertion point can be handy. While working on one section of a document you can scroll to view another section, and then with a single keystroke return to your original location.

You can greatly speed your work if you learn to scroll quickly and move the insertion point to any location you desire. Practice the various keystrokes and mouse actions, and soon they will become second nature.

SELECTING TEXT TO EDIT

As you edit a WordPerfect for Windows document, one technique that you'll find indispensable is *selecting text*, that is, marking the text that is to be affected by your next editing action. You can select any amount of text you wish, from a single character to an entire document by highlighting it on the screen. For example, in Figure 2.3 the first six words in the first sentence are selected.

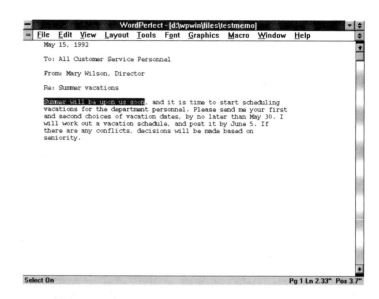

FIGURE 2.3:

Selected text is
highlighted on the
screen

TEXT SELECTION METHODS

There are three methods you can use for selecting text; one uses the mouse and two use the keyboard:

With the mouse: move the mouse I-beam pointer to one end of the text, drag the highlight to the other end of the text, and release the button.

With the keyboard (method 1): Move the insertion point to one end of the text, and then press and hold the Shift key. Use the movement keys to highlight the desired text, and then release the Shift key.

With the keyboard (method 2): Move the insertion point to one end of the text. Press and release the F8 key, and then use the movement keys to highlight the desired text.

To deselect text, press F8 or click anywhere on the screen.

In most cases, these three text selection methods produce identical results. There are a few differences, however. If you select text using the mouse or keyboard method 1, and then type any character, the selected text is deleted and replaced with that character. If you select text using keyboard method 2, and then type any character, the text selection expands to the next occurrence of that character in the document. Method 2 is a real timesaving feature, as you'll see next.

TEXT SELECTION SHORTCUTS

You can use several shortcuts to speed text selection. Some shortcuts rely on you pressing F8 to start selecting text (keyboard method 2), and then pressing any single character to automatically expand the selection to the next occurrence of that character in the document. Here are some examples:

- To select to the end of the current sentence, press F8 followed by a period.

- To select to the end of the current paragraph, press F8 followed by ↵.

- To select the next three words, press F8 followed by the spacebar 3 times.

Other shortcuts utilize the mouse (and a quick finger!):

- To select a word, *double-click* anywhere in the word. (Double-click means position the mouse pointer on the word, and then quickly press and release the left mouse button twice.)

- To select an entire sentence, triple-click anywhere in the sentence.

- To select an entire paragraph, quadruple-click (yes, that's four times!) anywhere in the paragraph.

You can see that there are many ways to select text. Use your practice memo to try out the various methods and timesaving shortcuts.

DELETING AND UNDELETING TEXT

It's a rare document that doesn't require some revision, and revisions almost always involve deleting some text. For a few characters, it's probably easiest to use the Del and Backspace keys, as you learned in the previous lesson. Remember, pressing Del deletes the one character to the right of the insertion point, and pressing Backspace deletes the one character to the left of the insertion point. For larger deletions, first select the text to be deleted, and then press Del or Backspace. The selected text is removed from the document, and the remaining text is automatically reformatted to fill in the space.

Let's give this a try, deleting the next to last sentence in the sample memo:

1. Move the insertion point to just before the next to last sentence.

2. Press F8, and then press . (period) to select the entire sentence. (You could also use one of the other text selection methods you have learned.)

3. Press Del.

RESTORING DELETED TEXT

What if you delete some text by mistake? Fortunately, WordPerfect for Windows can save you since it "remembers" the last three chunks of text you deleted. You can retrieve this text and insert it back into the document at the insertion point. Here's how:

1. Position the insertion point where you want the text replaced. This does not have to be the original location of the text.

2. Select Edit ➤ Undelete or press Alt+Shift+Backspace. The most recently deleted text is temporarily inserted in the document and highlighted, and a dialog box is displayed (see Figure 2.4).

3. In the dialog box, select Restore to replace the highlighted text in the document. Select Next or Previous to view other blocks of deleted text. Select Cancel to close the dialog box without undeleting any text.

TIP *If you delete several characters using Del or Backspace, WordPerfect for Windows considers it a single deletion. You can restore all the characters with one undelete command.*

Try the undelete procedure now with your sample memo, restoring the sentence you deleted in the previous section. You should restore it to its original location.

FIGURE 2.4:

The Undelete dialog box lets you recover deleted text, which is shown highlighted in the document

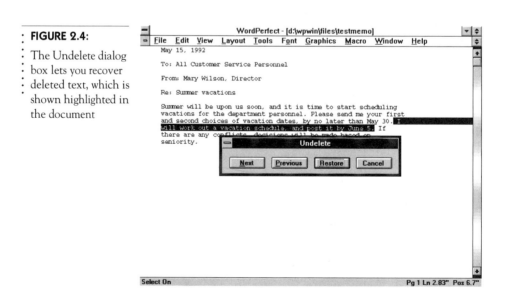

See the Undo entry in Part II.

COPYING AND MOVING TEXT

Editing a document often requires you to copy and move text from one location to another. The WordPerfect for Windows procedures for copying and moving text are almost identical. The difference is that after you copy text, the text exists in both the old and new locations. After you move text, it exists only in the new location and has been deleted from the old location.

Let's practice using the sample memo. Suppose you want to move the next to last sentence to the end of the memo, so it becomes the last sentence. These are the steps to follow:

1. Select the sentence.

2. Select Edit ➤ Cut, press Shift+Del, or click the Cut button on the Button Bar. (To copy the text, you would select Edit ➤ Copy, press Ctrl+Ins, or click the Copy button on the Button Bar.)

3. Press Ctrl+End to move the insertion point to the end of the document.

4. Select Edit ➤ Paste, press Shift+Ins, or click the Paste button on the Button Bar. The text is inserted at the insertion point.

As an alternate method of moving text, you can delete it, move the insertion point, and then undelete it.

When you select text and then cut or copy it, the text is moved or copied to a temporary storage location called the *clipboard*, replacing anything that was in the clipboard previously. Text in the clipboard can be pasted multiple times; however anything you cut or copy to the clipboard will remain there only until it is replaced by another cut or copy operation.

See the Appending Text entry in Part II.

SEARCHING FOR AND REPLACING TEXT

With WordPerfect for Windows it's a snap to search through your document for a specific word or phrase. You can simply search for text, or you can replace it with new text.

SEARCHING FOR TEXT

To search for text, you give WordPerfect for Windows a *template*, or model, of the text you are looking for. The program then searches your document, starting at the insertion point and moving either forward or backward.

You can specify whether the search is to proceed forward or backward from the insertion point. If you're not sure where the target lies in relation to the insertion point, it is a good idea to move the insertion point to the beginning of the document before searching.

We will practice searching by finding the word *vacation* in the memo. Here's what to do:

1. Press Ctrl+Home to move to the beginning of the document.

2. Select Edit ➤ Search, press F2, or click the Search button on the Button Bar. The Search dialog box, illustrated in Figure 2.5, is displayed.

3. Enter the search template **vacation** in the Search For text box.

4. Select Search or press ↵ to begin the search.

5. WordPerfect for Windows moves the insertion point just after the matching text.

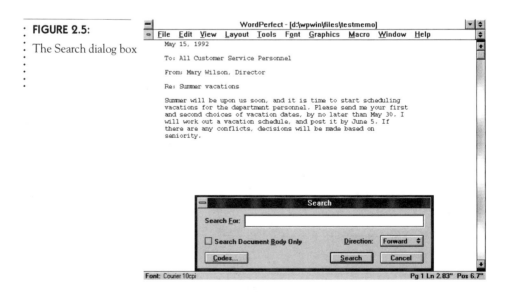

FIGURE 2.5:

The Search dialog box

To search again in the forward direction, select Edit ➤ Search Next or press Shift+F2.
To search backwards, select Edit ➤ Search Previous or press Alt+F2.

TIPS FOR SEARCHING

If you enter the search template in all lowercase letters, WordPerfect for Windows will find all occurrences of the text without regard to case. For example, a template of "texas" would find Texas, TEXAS, and texas. Uppercase letters in the template, however, will match only uppercase letters in the text. Thus, the template "Texas" will match Texas but not TEXAS or texas.

See the Word Count entry in Part II.

FINDING AND REPLACING TEXT

WordPerfect for Windows has a Replace command that lets you automatically go through your document replacing some or all occurrences of the *target text* with the specified *replacement text*. This can be a very handy editing tool. Suppose that you are writing a 100-page report on the ABC Corporation, and you learn that they just changed their name to XYZ Corporation. Rather than tediously going through the report changing every occurrence of "ABC" to "XYZ," you can make all needed changes in just a few seconds.

In many respects, Search and Replace works much like the Search command. The process moves either forward or backward from the insertion point. To search/replace in the entire document (which is what you'll want to do in most cases) move the insertion point to the start of the document first.

Using our sample memo, we will use the Search and Replace command to replace the word *seniority* with the phrase *length of service*. These are the steps to follow:

1. Press Ctrl+Home to move the insertion point to the start of the document.

2. Select Edit ➤ Replace or press Ctrl+F2. The Search and Replace dialog box is displayed (Figure 2.6).

3. Enter **seniority** in the Search For text box.

4. Enter **years of service** in the Replace With text box.

5. Select Search Next or press ↵ to start the process. WordPerfect for Windows finds and highlights the first occurrence of the target text. The dialog box remains displayed.

6. Select Replace to replace the highlighted occurrence of *seniority* with *years of service*. At this point you also have three other choices:

- ◆ Select Replace All to replace all remaining occurrences of the target text.
- ◆ Select Search Next to leave the highlighted occurrence of the target text unchanged, and then find the next.
- ◆ Select Close to end the search and replace operation.

WARNING

Be careful when using the Replace All command! You may get some unexpected results if you're not sure what your document contains.

You would repeat step 6 as many times as necessary. When the end of the document is reached, a message to that effect is displayed.

TIP

To simply delete occurrences of the target text, leave the Replace With text box blank.

FIGURE 2.6:

The Search and Replace dialog box

SAVING DOCUMENTS

You learned in the previous lesson that you must save your document on disk if you want to save it for future work sessions. This section covers saving documents in more detail.

A new document has no name until the first time you save it. At that point, you must assign it a name. Once a document has been named, you can save it under the existing name by selecting File ➤ Save, pressing Shift+F3, or clicking the Save button on the Button Bar.

You can also save a document under a different name. You might want to do this if you have modified the document and want to keep both the original and modified versions. Here's the procedure to follow:

1. Select File ➤ Save As or press F3.

2. The Save As dialog box is displayed with the document's current name in the Save As text box.

3. Type in the new document name, and then press ↵ or select Save.

When you use the Save As command to save a document under a new name, the original version with the original filename remains intact on disk.

You should now use the Save As command to save the modified version of the memo (remember, you moved one sentence to a new location). Assign the name NEW_MEMO to the modified document.

SUMMARY

This lesson taught you the basic skills you need to create a document in Word-Perfect for Windows: opening documents; entering, deleting, moving, and copying text; moving around documents; and saving documents. Practice to improve your skills; you now know enough to start doing some real work.

FOR MORE INFORMATION

You will find additional information about the topics covered in this lesson by consulting the following reference entries in Part II:

Copying Text

Deleting Text

Insertion Point

Moving Text

Opening a File

Saving a Document

Searching for and Replacing Text

Selecting Text

Undeleting Text

LESSON 3

*I*MPROVING YOUR DOCUMENT'S APPEARANCE — PART I

INTRODUCING

Basic formatting
Working with visible and invisible codes

While a document's contents are undoubtedly of primary importance, its appearance can have a significant effect on the clarity and impact of the information you are presenting. You can control the look of your documents by using the wide range of formatting commands offered by Word-Perfect for Windows. This lesson explains basic formatting; Lesson 4 discusses more complex formatting. If necessary, use the File ➤ Open command to open the document NEW_MEMO for use during this lesson.

FORMATTING CODES

Before getting to the "how-to" for formatting, you need to understand how Word-Perfect for Windows uses *formatting codes*. A formatting code is a special code that is placed in the document to control its format. Normally you don't see these codes, but only the results—that is, the formatting itself.

For example, suppose you underline a word in your document. WordPerfect for Windows inserts a "start underlining" code immediately before the word and a "stop underlining" code immediately after the word. Similarly, when you press ↵, a "hard return" code is inserted in the document. When you view or print the document, you see only the underlined word or the new line, not the codes; however, the codes are there, and they can be deleted, moved, and copied just like text.

TYPES OF CODES

Some formatting codes are inserted automatically by WordPerfect for Windows. A common example is the "soft return" code that is added when a line reaches the right margin. There are other codes you insert as you work on the document. These codes come in two basic types:

- ◆ Paired codes always operate together. One member of the pair turns a formatting feature on, and the second member turns it off. The underlining codes mentioned earlier are an example of paired codes.

- ◆ A single code operates alone. It is in effect from its location to the end of the document, or until another code takes effect. For example, if you change margins, a single "change margins" code will be inserted in the document. The new margins will be used from that point to the end of the document or until another "change margins" code is found.

VIEWING FORMATTING CODES

At times you will want to see the formatting codes in your document, particularly when you need to delete one or more codes. To view codes, select View ➤ Reveal Codes or press Alt+F3. The document window splits into two parts. The top part shows the document as you typed it, and the lower part shows the same section of the document with the formatting codes displayed (Figure 3.1).

Each code is enclosed in square brackets. Most codes are self-explanatory. Some use abbreviations: for example, [Hrt] for hard return and [Srt] for soft return. Go ahead and try revealing the hidden codes your sample document.

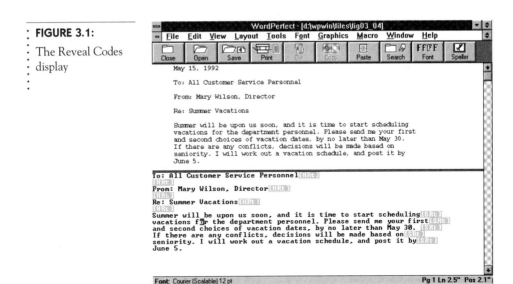

FIGURE 3.1:

The Reveal Codes
display

Now that you've seen how formatting codes work, we can get to the details of formatting your document. To close the Reveal Codes window, select View ➤ Reveal Codes or press Alt+F3.

INDENTATION

Indentation is the spacing between a paragraph's lines of text and the left and right margins. Several types of indentation are illustrated in Figure 3.2.

Indentation is usually applied to an entire paragraph. To indent an existing paragraph, move the insertion point to the left end of the first line, and then enter the desired indent command. To indent a new paragraph, press ↵ to start the paragraph, enter the desired indent command, and then start typing the paragraph. Here are the four indent commands:

Tab Indent	Press Tab. The first line is indented from the left margin.
Indent	Press F7. All lines are indented from the left margin.
Double indent	Press Ctrl+Shift+F7. All lines are indented from the left and right margins.
Hanging indent	Press Ctrl+F7. All lines except the first are indented from the left margin.

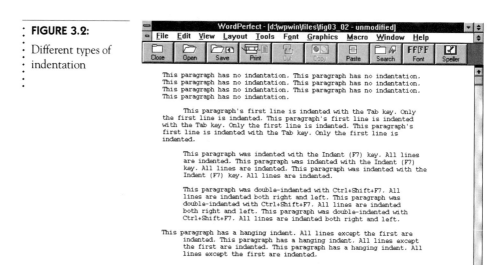

All of the indent commands (except Tab indent) can also be entered via the menus, by selecting Layout ➤ Paragraph, and then selecting the desired indent. The shortcut keys listed above are much faster, however.

Let's try a different indent style on our memo. We will apply double indentation to the main body of the memo. To do so, move the insertion point to the start of the first line (just before *Summer*), and then press Ctrl+Shift+F7. Your screen should now appear as in Figure 3.3.

Please see the Margins entry in Part II.

FIGURE 3.3:

A memo with the
main text double
indented

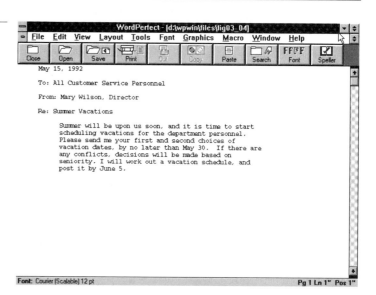

LINE SPACING

The line spacing setting controls the vertical distance between lines of text within your document. The default is 1, single spacing. You can set any line spacing you want, including fractional spacings such as 1.5. In our memo, let's change the line spacing to 2.

WARNING

Some printers cannot reproduce fractional line spacing.

1. Move the insertion point to where you want the new spacing to begin. In the memo this will be at the start of the main paragraph.

2. Select Layout ➤ Line or press Shift+F9.

3. Select Spacing. The Line Spacing dialog box is displayed, as shown in Figure 3.4.

4. Enter 2 in the text box. You can also use the ↑ and ↓ keys or click the up and down arrows next to the text box to increase or decrease the spacing by .5 at a time.

5. Select OK or press ↵. The document text is displayed with the specified spacing.

FIGURE 3.4:
The Line Spacing
dialog box

JUSTIFICATION

Justification refers to the way text is lined up at the left and right margins of the page. The default justification in WordPerfect for Windows is *left-justification*, meaning that text is aligned at the left margin, but it is not aligned (that is, it is *ragged*) at the right margin. You also have the options of right-justification (aligned right, ragged left), full-justification (aligned left and right), or center-justification (centered, ragged left and right). Figure 3.5 shows the four different justification options.
Let's change the memo to use full-justification:

1. Move the insertion point to the place where you want the new justification to start. In the memo, this will be the start of the main paragraph.

2. Select Layout ➤ Justification, and then select Full. The memo will now appear as in Figure 3.6.

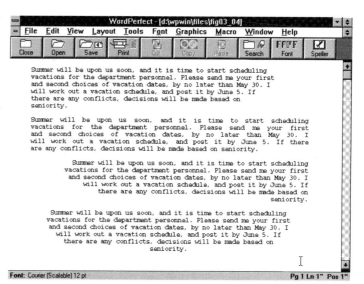

FIGURE 3.5:

Justification options: from top to bottom the paragraphs are left-justified (the default), full-justified, right-justified, and center-justified.

WARNING

Using full-justification with a monospaced font can result in uneven word spacing (as you see in Figure 3.6). Full-justification is best used with a proportional font.

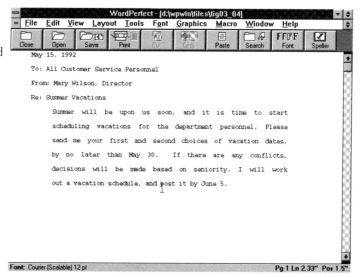

FIGURE 3.6:

The memo with the main text full-justified

TIP

To set justification quickly, use the shortcut keys: Ctrl+L (left), Ctrl+R (right), Ctrl+J (center), and Ctrl+F (full).

▌TALICS, BOLDFACE, AND UNDERLINING

Any text in your document can be displayed and printed in **boldface** or *italics*, or with an <u>underline.</u> You can even combine two or all of these attributes in the same text. Using different font attributes in your documents can be a great way to improve clarity and to call attention to important points.

You can assign the bold, italic, or underline attributes as you type, or you can assign them to existing text. You access the commands from the Font menu or use their shortcut keys:

Bold	Select Font ➤ Bold or press Ctrl+B
Italics	Select Font ➤ Italic or press Ctrl+I
Underline	Select Font ➤ Underline or press Ctrl+U

Let's use these commands to modify our memo. We want to use bold for the first four lines, and then add a new line at the end that is underlined. Here are the steps to follow:

1. Press Ctrl+Home to move the insertion point to the start of the document.

2. Press and hold Shift, and then press ↓ seven times to highlight the first four lines.

3. Select Font ➤ Bold or press Ctrl+B.

4. Press Ctrl+End to move the insertion point to the end of the document, and then press ↵ twice.

5. Select Font ➤ Underline or press Ctrl+U.

6. Type in the text: **Remember - May 30th at the latest!**

7. Select Font ➤ Underline or press Ctrl+U.

To remove all special attributes from text, select the text and choose Font ➤ Normal or press Ctrl+N.

Your memo should appear as in Figure 3.7. Now would be a good time to save the document since you've made several changes: Select File ➤ Save, press Shift+F3, or click Save on the Button Bar.

FIGURE 3.7:

The memo with bold and underlined text

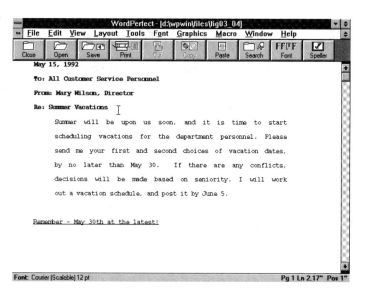

Please see the Subscript and Superscript and the Double Underline entries in Part II.

WORKING WITH CODES

To become adept at creating great-looking documents, you must become familiar with some of the finer points of using formatting codes.

DELETING CODES

If you want to remove special formatting from your document, you should delete the formatting codes. This is preferable to adding another code that cancels the first. You use the Reveal Codes window to delete codes: simply move the red cursor to the desired code and press Del. (On a monochrome monitor the cursor is displayed in reverse video.) If you delete one of a pair of codes, WordPerfect for Windows automatically deletes the second.

MOVING AND COPYING CODES

You can move and copy codes from one part of the document to another, just like you move and copy text. Codes can be moved/copied by themselves, but more often they are moved/copied along with some text.

There's no special trick to moving/copying codes. You simply must be sure that the codes are included in the selected text. The Reveal Codes window comes in handy here, as it shows you exactly where the insertion point is relative to the codes. Here's what to do:

1. Place the red Reveal Codes cursor on the first code you want included in the selection.

2. Press and hold Shift, and then move the cursor to the last code you want included in the selection.

3. Release Shift, and then select either Edit ➤ Cut or Edit ➤ Copy.

4. Move the insertion point to the new location, and then select Edit ➤ Paste or press Shift+Ins.

SEARCHING FOR AND REPLACING CODES

You can use the WordPerfect for Windows Search and Replace commands to find and optionally replace formatting codes in your document. Suppose you have written a report that uses bold for all of its headings. You suddenly decide you would rather use underlining for the headings. Instead of laboriously editing the entire document, you can use the Replace command to change all Bold formatting codes to Underline codes.

The following steps show you how to search for codes using the Edit ➤ Search command. (If you want to search for and replace codes using the Edit ➤ Replace command, the procedure is essentially identical except that you must enter replacement codes.) We will search our memo for the "full-justification" code, and then delete it to return the document to the default left-justification.

1. Move the insertion point to the start of the document.

2. Select Edit ➤ Search or press F2. The Search dialog box is displayed.

3. To enter one or more codes in the Search For text box, select the Codes command button. The Codes dialog box is displayed (Figure 3.8).

4. Scroll through the list of codes using the ↑, ↓, PgUp, PgDn, Home, and End keys, or using the mouse and scroll bar. Highlight the [Just] code and press ↵ or double-click the code.

5. Select Search or press ↵. WordPerfect for Windows moves the insertion point to the first occurrence of a Justification code in the document.

6. Press Alt+F3 to open the Reveal Codes window, and then press Backspace to delete the [Just:Full] code.

View ➤ Reveal Codes, p. 132

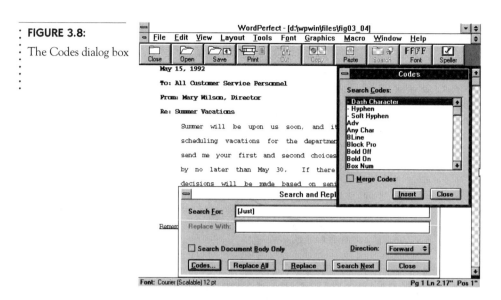

FIGURE 3.8:

The Codes dialog box

When you display the Codes dialog box, you'll see that there are dozens of different formatting codes. Most of them will be unfamiliar to you, but don't worry. As you continue to work with WordPerfect for Windows, you'll learn the ones you need. A list of the more frequently used formatting codes can be found in Part II under "Formatting Codes."

WARNING

You can search for any code, but you cannot replace with all codes. If you try to replace with one of these codes, you will receive an error message.

Before finishing this lesson, remember to save the memo.

SUMMARY

This lesson introduced the techniques of formatting a document. You learned about formatting codes, and how to control indentation, justification, and line spacing. You also learned how to display text in bold, italics, and underline, and how to search for and replace formatting codes.

FOR MORE INFORMATION

You will find additional information about the topics covered in this lesson by consulting the following reference entries in Part II:

Bold

Copying Text

Formatting Codes

Indentation

Italics

Justification

Line Spacing

Moving Text

Reveal Codes

Searching for and Replacing Text

Underline

LESSON 4

*I*MPROVING YOUR DOCUMENT'S APPEARANCE — PART II

INTRODUCING

Using Fonts and Font Attributes
Creating Headers and Footers

This lesson teaches you some additional document formatting commands. You'll learn how to use fonts, and how to add headers and footers to your documents. We will be using these techniques to further refine the appearance of our practice memo. If necessary, you should now use the File ➤ Open command to open the NEW_MEMO document.

USING FONTS

A *font* is a set of characters (letters, numbers, and so on) that have the same general design. Figure 4.1 shows some examples of different fonts and font sizes. WordPerfect for Windows gives you complete control over the fonts you use in your document.

NOTE

The number and types of fonts available to you depend on your printer. Your fonts may differ from the ones you'll see in this lesson.

FIGURE 4.1: Examples of fonts

CG Times 12 point

CG Times 36 point

`Courier 12 cpi`

Univers 12 point

Univers 18 point

Size
1 point = 1/72"
12 pt font = 1/6"

A font is identified by a name, such as Times Roman, Courier, or Swiss, and is typically available in various sizes. Font size is usually specified in terms of *points*, with 1 point equal to 1/72 inch. Thus, a 12-point font is approximately 1/6 inch high. Some fonts are measured in *cpi* (characters per inch), which gives the number of characters that fit into a horizontal inch.

TIP

As you work in a document, the name and size of the current font are displayed in the status bar.

THE INITIAL FONT

Every document has an *initial font* that is used for all parts of the document unless you make font changes. The default initial font is Courier 12 point (or your printer's equivalent), unless you specified a different initial font when you installed WordPerfect for Windows.

Note that the initial font is applied to all parts of the document: the text itself, headers, footers, page numbers, and everything else. If you want to change the font for the entire document, change the initial font. If you want to change the font for a restricted portion of the document, change the font within the document.

When you change the initial font, the location of the insertion point does not matter. The font change automatically affects the entire document.

Let's change the initial font for our memo:

1. Select Layout ➤ Document or press Ctrl+Shift+F9.

2. Select Initial Font. The Document Initial Font dialog box is displayed (Figure 4.2). In the Font and Point Size list boxes, the name and size of the current initial font are highlighted. The lower box shows a sample of text in that font and size.

3. Select a different font name and/or size. The sample box shows you how it will look. For the memo select CG Times (Scalable) and a size of 12 points. If this font is not on your list, select another font name.

4. Select OK or press ↵. The document is displayed in the selected font.

For some fonts the size is part of the font name. When you highlight one of these fonts, the Point Size dialog box is empty.

FIGURE 4.2:

The Document Initial Font dialog box

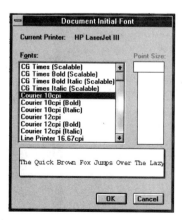

CHANGING THE FONT IN PART OF A DOCUMENT

You can use a different font for a portion of the document. If you change the font when text is selected, the new font will be used for that text only. Otherwise, the new font applies from the location of the insertion point onward.

To see how to change the font of part of a document, we will make a further modification to the memo. We'll change the font of the memo's main paragraph:

1. Select the paragraph.

2. Select Font ➤ Font or press F9. The Font dialog box is displayed (Figure 4.3).

3. In the Font and Point Size list boxes, select the name and size of the new font. The lower box shows a sample of text in the selected font and size. For the memo select Univers (Scalable), 12 point. If that font is not available, select another 12-point font.

4. Select OK or press ↵.

When you change fonts using the Font command, a font change code is inserted in the document. You can change fonts anywhere, even in the middle of a line or word.

CHANGING FONT SIZE

WordPerfect for Windows lets you change the size of text in your document without actually changing the font itself. You have five choices; from smallest to largest they are Fine, Small, Large, Very Large, and Extra Large. These sizes are always based on the current font. For example, if the current font is Times Roman 12 point, text with the size attribute "Large" would print as Times Roman 14 point. If

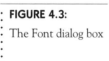

FIGURE 4.3:

The Font dialog box

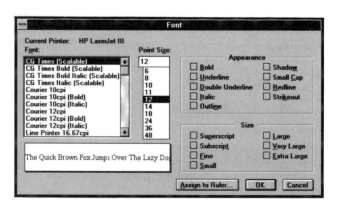

you later change the document's initial font to Swiss 14 point, the "Large" text would print as Swiss 16 point.

WARNING

The font and font sizes that are available depend on your printer, and may be different from those you see here. Experiment to determine your printer's capabilities.

As with other formatting changes, you can apply size attributes to text as you type or to selected text. We will use the latter technique to display the last sentence in our memo in larger type:

1. Select the last sentence in the memo (the one that's underlined).
2. Select Font ➤ Size or press Ctrl+S. The Size menu is displayed (Figure 4.4)
3. Select the desired size. For the memo select Very Large.
4. Select OK or press ↵. After pressing Home to deselect the sentence, your memo should appear as in Figure 4.5.

TIP

When you want text to be in a different size from the rest of the document, but you want to use the same font, it is always better to use the size attributes instead of changing the font itself.

HEADERS AND FOOTERS

A *header* or *footer* is text that is repeated at the top or bottom of every page in a document. They can be particularly useful for longer documents, serving to identify the document and perhaps indicating the chapter number and page number. In headers and footers you can use just about any WordPerfect for Windows feature,

---

FIGURE 4.4:

The Size menu offers you five text size attributes

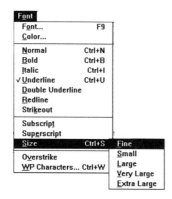

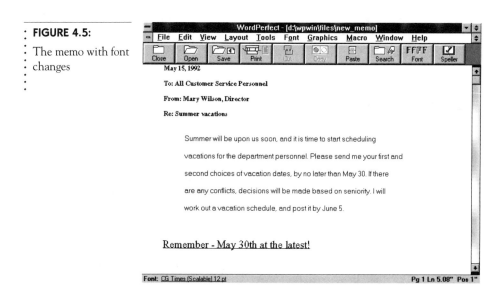

FIGURE 4.5:
The memo with font changes

such as font changes and justification. This section shows you how to create a footer; the procedures for headers are identical.

CREATING A HEADER OR FOOTER

You can define two different footers, called Footer A and Footer B (you can also define two headers, A and B). With two footers you can have different footers on odd and even numbered pages.

Headers and footers do not display on the editing screen. To view them, you must use the Print Preview feature, covered in Lesson 6.

The following steps show you how to add a footer. Let's add a footer to the memo:

1. Move the insertion point to the first page where you want the footer to appear. For our single-page memo this step can be ignored.

2. Select Layout ➤ Page or press Alt+F9.

3. Select Footers (or, to create a header, select Headers). The Footers dialog box is displayed (Figure 4.6).

4. Select Footer A if you are creating the document's first footer. Select Footer B only if you are creating a second footer for alternate pages.

5. Select Create. The footer editing screen opens, as shown in Figure 4.7. This screen is similar to the normal editing screen, and almost all editing commands function in the same way.

6. Type in the footer text. For the memo type **From the desk of Mary Wilson.**

7. Select Close.

FIGURE 4.6:

The Footers
dialog box

FIGURE 4.7:

The footer
editing screen

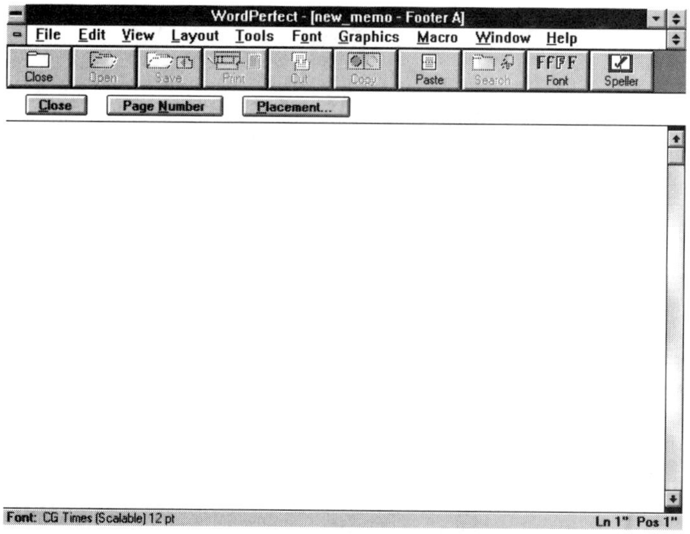

You can use the Font command to specify the font to be used within the footer itself. If you do not, the footer uses the font that is current at the location where the footer is created.

See the Endnotes and Footnotes entries in Part II.

EDITING A HEADER OR FOOTER

You can make changes to an existing header or footer at any time. If your document contains only a single footer, the insertion point can be at any location when you edit the footer. If there are multiple footers, the first footer behind the insertion point will be edited. If no footer is found behind the insertion point, the first one in front of the insertion point will be edited.

Let's edit the footer in our memo, adding the title Ms. to Mary Wilson's name. Here's how:

1. Select Layout ➤ Page or press Alt+F9.

2. Select Footers (or, to edit a header, select Headers). The Footer dialog box is displayed.

3. Select Footer A.

4. Select Edit. The footer editing screen opens with the existing footer displayed.

5. Make the desired change in the footer (that is, type **Ms.** before *Mary*), and then select Close.

You're finished modifying the memo for now, so you should save it.

It's important to understand that editing a footer changes all occurrences of the footer. If you create a footer on page 1, and then edit it on page 10, the footers on pages 1–9 (and all other pages) will be changed. If you want to change the text in a header from a particular page forward, move the insertion point to that page and create a new footer. For example, suppose you are writing a long document with several chapters. Create a Footer A that reads "Chapter 1" at the start of the first chapter, and then create another Footer A that reads "Chapter 2" at the start of the second chapter, and so on.

DISCONTINUING A HEADER OR FOOTER

You can discontinue a header or footer at any point in the document, preventing it from printing on subsequent pages. For example, you might want a footer to print on all pages in the body of a document but not on the index pages at the end of the document. To discontinue a footer:

1. Move the insertion point to the first page where the footer is to be discontinued.

2. Select Layout ➤ Page or press Alt+F9.

3. Select Footers (or Headers).

4. Select the Footer, A or B, to discontinue.

5. Select Discontinue.

 Once a header or footer has been discontinued, you cannot simply "re-continue" it on later pages. You must create a new header or footer.

The location of the insertion point will affect how creating, editing, and discontinuing footers work. For example, in a 20-page document, let's say you create footer A with the insertion point on page 1. Then, with the insertion point on page 10:

◆ If you create a new footer A, the original footer will be printed on pages 1–9 and the new footer on pages 10–20.

◆ If you edit footer A, the edited footer will be printed on all pages 1–20.

◆ If you discontinue footer A, the original footer will be printed on pages 1–9 and no footer will be printed on 10–20.

SUMMARY

In this lesson you learned some more complex formatting techniques: using different fonts in your documents, controlling font size, and adding headers and footers to a document.

FOR MORE INFORMATION

You will find additional information about the topics covered in this lesson by consulting the following reference entries in Part II:

Font

Headers and Footers

Initial Font

LESSON 5

CONTROLLING
THE PAGE LAYOUT

INTRODUCING

Page breaks and page numbers
Setting Margins
Paper type

This lesson covers commands that affect the way text is laid out on the page. Page layout is a part of formatting, and it is important in creating attractive documents. You will create a new document to use for practice in this lesson.

STARTING A NEW PAGE

A *page break* marks the location where one page ends and the next page begins. When one page is full, WordPerfect for Windows inserts a soft page break code [Spg] in the text. If you later add or delete text, the soft page break codes are repositioned, if necessary, to keep the page breaks at the proper locations. On the editing screen a soft page break is indicated by a single horizontal line.

hard page break
Ctrl + ↵
indicated by =

At times you may need to control the location of page breaks. For example, you might want each chapter of a manuscript to begin on a new page even if the previous page is not full. You do this by pressing Ctrl+↵ to insert a hard page break code [Hpg]. Hard page break codes are never moved, but always remain in the same position relative to the text immediately preceding and following. On the editing screen a hard page break is indicated by a double horizontal line.

NOTE

Please see the Conditional End of Page and Block Protect entries in Part II.

Enter the document shown in Figure 5.1. Start with a blank screen, and type it in as shown. After the word "Furniture" in the closing, press Ctrl+↵ to start a new page, and then type in the remainder of the text.
When you have finished entering the document, check it for mistakes, and then save it to disk using the name QUOTE.

FIGURE 5.1:

A document that uses a hard page break

WordPerfect - [d:\wpwin\files\fig5_1 - unmodified]
File Edit View Layout Tools Font Graphics Macro Window Help
Close Open Save Print Cut Copy Paste Search Font Speller

June 10, 1992

Arthur Jones
Jones, Smith, and Haggerty
123 East End Avenue
Oakland, NJ 07436

Dear Mr. Jones:

I am pleased to respond to your request for prices on furniture
for your offices. Attached you will find an itemized quotation.
This quote is good until July 15th.

Yours truly,

Andrea Carson, Vice President
Acme Office Furniture

QUOTATION - June 10, 1992

One teak executive conference table..........$3,500.00
Ten teak swivel chairs @ $400.00..............4,000.00
One teak credenza............................2,600.00

Total, including delivery..................$10,100.00

Font: Courier 10cpi Pg 1 Ln 1" Pos 1"

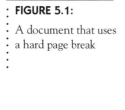

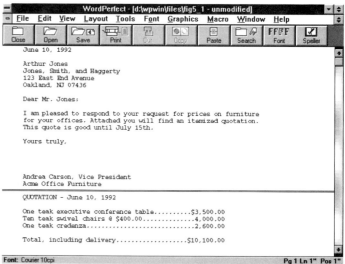

SETTING MARGINS

A *margin* is the distance between the edge of the page and your text. Each page has four margins: left, right, top, and bottom. You can control each margin individually.

LEFT AND RIGHT MARGINS

The left and right margins are measured in inches from the edge of the page. The default setting for both is one inch. When you change left and/or right margins, the change is effective from the location of the insertion point on. If you change margins while the insertion point is within a paragraph, the new margin code will be placed at the start of that paragraph.

Changing margins has a similar effect to changing indentation. You can often use the two interchangeably. Generally speaking, though, you should use indentation for small sections of text (a paragraph or two), and margin changes for larger sections of text.

Let's change the left margin on the second page of our document so that the quotation is offset by 2 inches from the left edge of the paper:

1. Move the insertion point to the beginning of the line that starts "One teak executive…"
2. Select Layout ➤ Margins or press Ctrl+F8. The Margins dialog box is displayed (see Figure 5.2).
3. Enter 2 in the Left text box. You can also use the ↑ and ↓ keys to increase or decrease the margin setting by 0.01".
4. Select OK or press ↵. The document will now appear as in Figure 5.3.

TOP AND BOTTOM MARGINS

The top and bottom margins specify the amount of blank space at the top and bottom of each page. You use the same technique to change these margins as you do

FIGURE 5.2:

The Margins dialog box

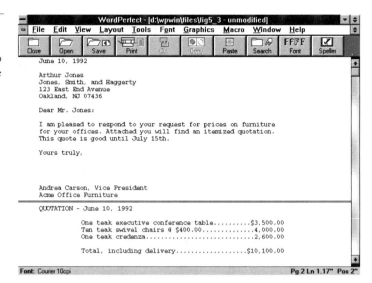

for the left and right margins. When you change top and/or bottom margins, the formatting code is placed at the top of the current page. Note that the top and bottom margin settings affect the placement of headers and footers.

WARNING

Some printers require a minimum margin setting because they are not able to print to the edge of the paper. If you try to set a margin that is less than the allowed minimum for your printer, WordPerfect for Windows will inform you.

PAGE NUMBERS

WordPerfect for Windows keeps track of page numbers, and displays the current page number on the status bar. You can also have page numbers print as part of the document. Let's add page numbers to our document:

1. Move the insertion point to the first page where you want the page numbers to begin. For our example this is the first page.

2. Select Layout ➤ Page or press Alt+F9.

3. Select Numbering. The Page Numbering dialog box is displayed (Figure 5.4).

4. Select the Position pop-up list. This list includes all the page number position options, with a checkmark next to the one currently in effect. From the list select the Bottom Center option. The two miniature pages display how the selected position option will look.

5. Select OK or press ↵.

FIGURE 5.4:

The Page Numbering dialog box

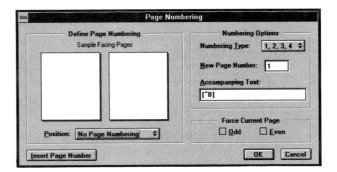

To turn off page numbering, display the Page Numbering dialog box and select No Page Numbering from the Position pop-up list.

Page numbers are printed, but they do not display on the editing screen. To view them, you must use the Print Preview feature, covered in the next lesson.

WordPerfect for Windows normally counts pages sequentially from the start of the document. To reset page numbering:

1. Move the insertion point to the page you want to assign a new number.

2. Select Layout ➤ Page or press Alt+F9, and then select Numbering. The Page Numbering dialog box is displayed.

3. Enter the desired page number in the New Page Number text box.

4. Select OK or press ↵.

When you reset page numbers, the specified page number is assigned to the current page and following pages are numbered sequentially starting with that number.

CENTERING TEXT TOP TO BOTTOM

Certain document pages, such as a title page, look better if they are centered between the top and bottom edges of the paper. WordPerfect for Windows can do this automatically, letting you avoid the hassle of inserting the proper number of blank lines to center text on a page.

You will not see the effect of page centering during editing, but the text will be centered when printed and on the Print Preview screen.

Centering a page vertically makes no sense unless the page contains fewer lines than a normal full page. This means that a page to be centered is usually separated from the previous and subsequent pages by hard page breaks. We will use the center page command to center the text on the second page of our document:

1. Press Ctrl+End followed by Alt+Home to move the insertion point to the start of the second page.

2. Select Layout ➤ Page or press Alt+F9.

3. Select Center Page.

WARNING

The Center Page command may not work properly unless the insertion point is at the beginning of the page.

CHANGING PAPER TYPE

Unless you tell it otherwise, WordPerfect for Windows assumes that your document will be printed on standard $8\frac{1}{2} \times 11$-inch paper. There may be times when you want to print on another paper size, or need to orient the print differently on the page. For instance, you may want to print envelopes or use $8\frac{1}{2} \times 14$-inch legal size paper.

WordPerfect for Windows has several predefined paper types that will meet most needs. Each "type" is a definition that includes information such as paper size and orientation. You need to understand the components of a paper type definition to be able to select them properly. The aspects of a paper type definition that you'll need to know are as follows:

- Size gives the dimensions of the paper, in inches. The horizontal measurement is always listed first. Thus, dimensions of 8.5×11 refers to paper that is 8.5 inches wide and 11 inches long.

- Orientation specifies how the print is placed on the paper. The default *portrait* orientation prints lines of text parallel to the short edge of the paper. *Landscape* orientation prints lines of text parallel to the long edge of the paper. Landscape orientation is not available on some printers. WordPerfect for Windows uses small graphics icons, or symbols, on the screen to represent different orientations.

- Location tells the printer where to get the paper. *Contin* (for continuous) refers to your printer's usual paper source: tractor-feed paper or a sheet feeder for dot-matrix printers; the paper cassette for laser printers. *Manual* specifies that individual pages are hand-fed to the printer.

◆ The Prompt setting is either Yes or No. If set to Yes, the program pauses before printing each page and prompts you to insert a sheet of paper. Use a prompt setting of Yes to manually feed single items, such as envelopes and letterhead stationery, to your printer.

Unless you are changing the paper type on the first page of a document, it's a good idea to insert a hard page break just before the paper type code.

When you change paper type in a document, it takes effect with the current page. The following steps show you how to change the paper type for our sample document to $8^{1}/_{2} \times 14$-inch legal:

1. Press Ctrl+Home to move the insertion point to the start of the document.

2. Select Layout ➤ Page or press Alt+F9.

3. Select Paper Size. The Paper Size dialog box is displayed, as shown in Figure 5.5. The current paper type is highlighted in the list; it should be Standard 8.5" × 11".

4. Use the mouse and scroll bar, or the PgUp, PgDn, ↑, and ↓ keys to scroll through the list of paper types. Move the highlight to Legal 8.5" × 14". (If your paper type list does not include this size, select the closest alternative.)

5. Press ↵ or select OK.

When you change paper type, WordPerfect for Windows automatically changes formatting (if necessary) to take the new paper size into account. For our practice document you won't see any changes, however.

Since we don't really want the practice document on legal size paper, you should delete the paper size code. It will be located near the beginning of the document and will read [Paper Sz/Typ:8.5" × 14",Legal]. (Remember to use the Reveal

---

FIGURE 5.5:

The Paper Size dialog box

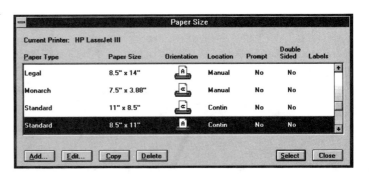

Codes screen!) Deleting this code will return the document to the default 8.5 × 11-inch paper size. You should save the practice document now, before going on to the next lesson.

SUMMARY

In this lesson you learned how to control the page layout of your document. Setting margins, centering top-to-bottom, and controlling page breaks are all important formatting techniques. You also saw how WordPerfect for Windows can work with a variety of paper types and sizes.

FOR MORE INFORMATION

You will find additional information about the topics covered in this lesson by consulting the following reference entries in Part II:

Center Page

Hard Page Break

Margins

Page Numbering

Paper Size

LESSON 6

*P*RINTING YOUR DOCUMENT

INTRODUCING

Previewing printer output
Printing an entire document
Printing part of a document

WordPerfect for Windows provides a variety of printing options that cover just about any circumstance. To print any document, you must have selected and installed a printer when you installed WordPerfect for Windows on your computer. If necessary, open the file QUOTE that you created in the previous lesson.

PREVIEWING THE PRINT JOB

Before actually printing your document, you may want to see a preview of the final printout. The WordPerfect for Windows print preview feature can save you lots of time and paper that would otherwise be wasted fine-tuning the appearance of a printed document.

You may be thinking that a special preview is not needed. Doesn't the Word-Perfect for Windows normal editing screen show you how your document will look when printed? Well, yes and no. The editing screen is very similar to the final printed page, but it is not identical. For example, the editing screen cannot show a full page, nor does it display headers, footers, or page numbers. For an accurate picture of what your printout will look like, you must use the preview feature.

To preview the current document, select File ➤ Preview or press Shift+F5. The Print Preview screen opens and displays the current document page (Figure 6.1).

Lines of text may display as solid black bars on the print preview screen (as in Figure 6.1). You cannot read the text but you can see how it is arranged on the page.

Look at Figure 6.1 and note the following components of the Print Preview screen:

♦   The menu bar has pull-down menus that you use when working on the Print Preview screen.

FIGURE 6.1:

The Print Preview window

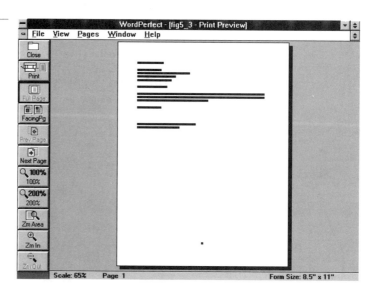

- The Button Bar, displayed down the left side of the screen, contains buttons for some of the more frequently needed print preview commands.

- The status bar at the bottom of the screen displays the scale, page number, and form size of the page in view. The *scale* is the size of the screen image relative to the final printed page. For example, 100% is actual printed size, and 50% is one-half of printed size.

When you first display the Print Preview screen, the Scale setting that is in effect will depend on your document and also on previous use of the preview feature. Your screen may not look quite like Figure 6.1.

The Print Preview menus and Button Bar work the same as the regular menus and Button Bar.

PRINT PREVIEW VIEWING OPTIONS

The View menu contains commands that control the way the preview is displayed. You use these commands to zoom in on a small part of the document or to view an entire page. Use low scale factors to view large areas with less detail; use high scale factors to view small areas with more detail.

- The 100% command displays the page at 100% scale.

- The 200% command displays the page at 200% scale.

- The Zoom In command increases the scaling by 25%.

- The Zoom Out command decreases the scaling by 25%.

- The Zoom Area command lets you zoom in on a selected area. When you choose this command, a pair of crosshairs is displayed on the screen. Use the mouse to move the crosshairs to one corner of the area to be viewed. Then press and hold the mouse button, drag the outline to the opposite corner, and release the button. Figure 6.2 shows the display zoomed to cover the upper-left corner of our document.

- The Zoom to Full Width command displays the entire width of the page.

- The Reset command returns the display to the default scale.

When the page is enlarged on the preview screen, you can use the *panning* feature to quickly move the view to different portions of the page. Panning is available only if both vertical and horizontal scroll bars are displayed at the edges of the preview page (as in Figure 6.2). You can pan in any direction by using the mouse and scroll bars, or by pressing the arrow keys. You can also pan directly to a specific location using the mouse:

1. Move the mouse pointer to any location on the page, and click. The pointer changes to a four-headed arrow, and a miniature version of the current page is displayed with a box outlining the portion of the page that is currently in view. (See Figure 6.3.)

2. Click anywhere on the miniature page to pan the display to that location. Or, drag the box to the desired location on the miniature page.

FIGURE 6.2:

The display has been zoomed to enlarge a portion of the preview display

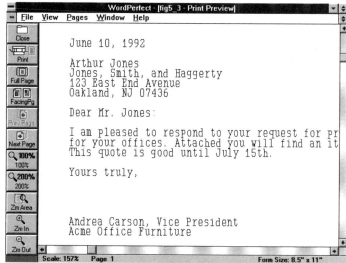

FIGURE 6.3:

Panning to a different region of the page

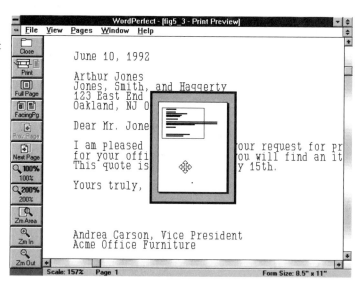

3. To cancel the panning action, click anywhere outside the miniature page or press Esc.

You should spend a little time trying these view commands with your document to get a feel for how they work. Remember, nothing you do on the Print Preview screen can affect the contents or formatting of your document.

PRINT PREVIEW PAGE OPTIONS

The commands on the Pages menu control which page or pages you view on the Print Preview screen.

- ◆ Select Full Page to view a single full page.

- ◆ Select Facing Pages to view two facing pages. Even-numbered pages are displayed on the left, and odd-numbered pages on the right. The Facing pages display is shown in Figure 6.4.

- ◆ Select Prev Page or Next Page to view the previous or next page.

- ◆ Select Go To Page to view a specific page. When you select this command, a dialog box opens. Enter the desired page number and press ↵.

The Facing Pages display always shows an even-numbered page on the left and an odd-numbered page on the right. Your practice document does not have facing pages, so it cannot be displayed in this manner.

FIGURE 6.4:

Use the Facing Pages command to preview two pages at once

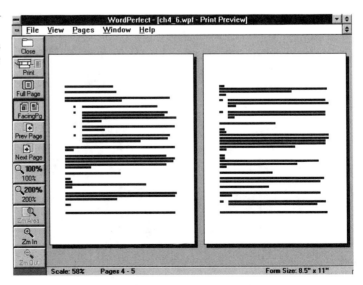

By using the Print Preview feature, you can insure that your document will print as desired without wasting time and paper on test print runs. After experimenting with the Pages commands, you should press Ctrl+F4 or click the Close button to close the preview screen.

PRINTING THE ENTIRE DOCUMENT

After you have previewed your document and determined that it is ready to print, you can print the entire document quickly. The following steps show you how to print a copy of our practice document, QUOTE:

1. Select File ➤ Print, press F5, or click the Print button on the Button Bar. The Print dialog box is displayed (Figure 6.5).

2. Select Print or press ↵ to print the entire document. (You'll learn about some of the settings in this dialog box later.)

To print directly from the Print Preview screen, click the Print button, select File ➤ Print, or press F5.

TIP

WordPerfect for Windows displays the Current Print Job dialog box showing progress in preparing the document for printing. Select Cancel Print Job to abort printing. Once this status box is closed, you can return to working as the printing takes place. You can continue to edit the document, but changes made now will not be present in the printout.

FIGURE 6.5:

The Print dialog box

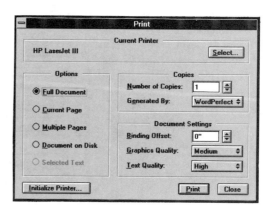

PRINTING PART OF A DOCUMENT

There will be times when you need to print only a portion of a document. Word-Perfect for Windows gives you several choices.

PRINTING THE CURRENT PAGE

To print the current page (the page containing the insertion point):

1. Select File ➤ Print, press F5, or click the Print button on the Button Bar. The Print dialog box is displayed.

2. Select Current Page from the Options section of the dialog box.

3. Select Print or press ↵.

PRINTING A RANGE OF PAGES

You can also print a specified range of pages:

1. Select File ➤ Print, press F5, or click the Print button on the Button Bar. The Print dialog box is displayed.

2. Select Multiple Pages from the Options section of the dialog box.

3. Select Print or press ↵. The Multiple Pages dialog box is displayed (Figure 6.6).

4. Enter the desired page range in the Range text box.

5. Select Print or press ↵.

FIGURE 6.6:

The Multiple Pages dialog box

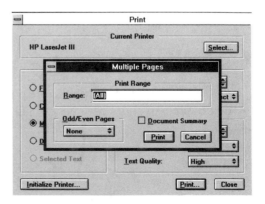

When entering a page range in the Multiple Pages dialog box, use the formats shown in these examples:

1–5	Pages 1 through 5.
1, 3, 5	Pages 1, 3, and 5.
1–5,10–15	Pages 1 through 5 and 10 through 15.
1–5,7	Pages 1 through 5 and page 7.

Please see the Page Numbering entry in Part II.

If you use the New Page Number command (covered in Lesson 5) to reset page numbering in your document, WordPerfect for Windows treats the document as consisting of a number of sections. Section 1 is from the beginning of the document up to the first New Page Number code, section 2 is from the first to the second New Page Number code, and so on. When specifying pages to print, enter the section number first, followed by a colon and the page(s). If you do not specify a section, the first section is assumed:

2:1–5	Pages 1 through 5 in section 2.
1–5,2:7	Pages 1 through 5 in section 1 and page 7 in section 2.

To print selected text: select the text, display the Print dialog box, and then press ↵.

SUMMARY

This lesson showed you how to create printouts of your documents. You learned that you can print an entire document or just a selected portion. You also learned how to use the Print Preview feature to see how your printout will look.

FOR MORE INFORMATION

You will find additional information about the topics covered in this lesson by consulting the following reference entries in Part II:

Print Preview

Printing Files

LESSON 7

USING MACROS TO SAVE TIME

INTRODUCING

Creating, recording, and replaying macros

This lesson teaches you how to use macros. The subject could occupy an entire book, so this lesson will cover just the basics. Even limited to the basics, however, you'll find that macros can be great timesavers. The first part of this lesson explains some macro fundamentals. Then, later in the lesson, you'll create your own macro.

WHAT IS A MACRO?

A *macro* is a series of recorded keystrokes and commands that instructs Word-Perfect for Windows to perform a particular task. When you want the task performed, you replay the macro rather than doing the required actions and entering the commands yourself. Macros are ideal for tasks that you perform regularly: they not only save time but reduce the chance of errors.

A macro can contain the following items:

- Text that becomes part of your document

- Any WordPerfect for Windows commands such as those for formatting, printing, and saving a document

- Special programming commands

Special programming commands are an advanced feature that is beyond the scope of this book. If you're interested, please refer to your WordPerfect for Windows documentation. However, you can create many powerful macros without programming commands.

How do you create a macro? You first tell WordPerfect for Windows to start recording, and then you perform the actions and enter the text you want in the macro. When you are finished, stop recording. The macro is saved, available for replay at anytime.

RECORDING A MACRO

When you record a macro, you perform the actual actions that you want the macro to contain. These actions will have their usual effects on the current document. You also assign a name to the macro so you can replay it later. These are the steps to follow:

1. Select Macro ➤ Record or press Ctrl+F10. The Record Macro dialog box is displayed, as shown in Figure 7.1.

2. In the Filename text box enter a one- to eight- character name for the macro. Do not add an extension to the macro filename—WordPerfect for Windows automatically adds the WCM extension. (See the section below on replaying macros for information on a filenaming convention you can use to make playback even simpler.)

3. In the Descriptive Name text box enter a brief description of the macro's purpose. Entering a description is optional but advisable.

4. In the Abstract text box you can enter a more lengthy description of the macro. This too is optional, but it is a good idea for long, complicated macros.

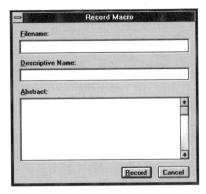

5. Select Record or press ⏎. You are returned to the editing screen. Enter the text and commands that you want in the macro. While a macro is recording, the status bar displays "Recording Macro." In addition, the mouse pointer displays as a "no" symbol (a circle with a diagonal line through it) when it's in the text area of the screen. This is to remind you that while recording a macro, you cannot use the mouse to move the insertion point or to scroll (although you can use it to select commands). You must use the keyboard to move the insertion point while recording a macro.

6. When you have completed the desired actions, select Macro ➤ Stop or press Ctrl+Shift+F10. Macro recording stops, the macro is saved, and you are returned to normal editing mode.

REPLAYING A MACRO

When you replay a macro, the effect on your document is exactly the same as if you had entered the macro's commands directly. Here's how to replay a macro:

1. Select Macro ➤ Play or press Alt+F10. The Play Macro dialog box is displayed (Figure 7.2).

2. If you know the name of the macro, you can type it into the Filename text box. Otherwise, select the macro name from the Files list box.

3. Press ⏎ or select Play. The macro is replayed.

WARNING

Before replaying an untested macro, you should save your document just in case a problem arises.

FIGURE 7.2:

The Play Macro
dialog box

There's a shortcut you can use to replay macros that you use frequently. First, you must assign a special filename to the macro when you first record it. The special name takes the form CTRL or CTRLSFT plus a single letter or numeral. For example, you can use CTRLA, CTRLSFTX, CTRL6, CTRLSFT4, and so on. To assign these names, press the corresponding key combination while the Filename text box is active in the Record Macro dialog box. You can name the macro two ways: you can type **C-T-R-L**-*letter* (or **C-T-R-L-S-F-T**-*letter*), or you can press Ctrl-*letter* (or Ctrl-Shift-letter). Then to replay the macro, simply press Ctrl+*letter* or Ctrl+Shift+*letter*. For example, to replay the macro named CTRLA, you would press Ctrl+A.

WARNING

You should avoid assigning Ctrl+letter names to macros because many Ctrl+letter combinations are already assigned to WordPerfect for Windows commands. For example, pressing Ctrl+I will execute the italics command and not any macro you may have assigned to Ctrl+I. You could, however, still play the macro with the Macro ➤ Play command.

A MACRO EXAMPLE

If you're still a bit unsure about macros, working through an example will help make things clear. We will record a macro that creates the template for a business letter: the date, return address, closing, and so on.

PLANNING THE MACRO

For all but the simplest macros, it's a good idea to do a little planning before actually starting. For our business letter template we want the following items:

- ◆ The current date and our return address in the upper-right corner.
- ◆ A closing with our name, title, and space for a signature.
- ◆ When the macro is finished replaying, the cursor should be placed at the proper location to enter the recipient's address.

To place today's date in a document, select Tools ➤ Date Text or press Ctrl+F5.

The finished template is shown in Figure 7.3.

Please see the Date entry in Part II.

RECORDING THE MACRO

Let's record the macro for our business letter template:

1. Start with a blank document screen. Select Macro ➤ Record or press Ctrl+F10. The Record Macro dialog box is displayed.

2. In the Filename text box enter a descriptive name for the macro, such as BUS_LET, and then press ↵. You are now in macro recording mode.

3. Press ↵ once to place a blank line at the top of the template. Then press Tab eight times followed by Ctrl+F5 to insert the date near the right margin. *Tools ➤ Date ➤ Text (p.118) for Today's date*

4. Press ↵ twice. Enter the address as shown, with each line preceded by eight tabs. *Tools ➤ Date ➤ code for current date*

5. After typing the zip code, press ↵ seven times.

6. Enter the salutation **Yours truly**, press ↵ six times, and then enter your name and title.

7. Press ↑ ten times to move the cursor up to where the recipient's address will be added.

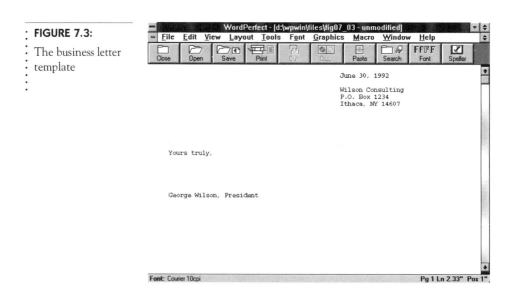

FIGURE 7.3:

The business letter template

8. The template is now complete. Select Macro ➤ Stop or press Ctrl+Shift+F10 to stop recording.

The macro is saved on disk, and can be replayed at any time you are starting a business letter.

REPLAYING THE MACRO

To replay any macro, you must first get your document to the proper state. Our macro is intended to be replayed on a blank document screen. To clear the screen, select File ➤ Close, and then answer No when WordPerfect for Windows asks if you want to save the document. Then:

1. Select Macro ➤ Play or press Alt+F10. The Play Macro dialog box is displayed.

2. In the Filename text box, type the name of the macro (BUS_LET or whatever name you assigned). You can also select the name from the Files list.

3. Select Play or press ↵. The macro will play and the letter template will be created on your screen just as if you had typed it yourself. Once the macro is finished, continue working on the letter as usual.

Since you don't need to save this document, clear the screen by selecting File ➤ Close, and then answering No to the prompt.

SUMMARY

This lesson has introduced you to WordPerfect for Windows macros, a powerful feature that you can use to automate many repetitive document tasks. You learned what a macro is, how to record a macro, and how to replay a macro; however, this lesson really only scratched the surface of macros. If you want to learn more about them, please refer to your WordPerfect for Windows documentation. You can also experiment with the sample macros that are provided with your WordPerfect for Windows package.

FOR MORE INFORMATION

You will find additional information about the topics covered in this lesson by consulting the following reference entries in Part II:

Date

Macro

LESSON 8

OTHER FEATURES

INTRODUCING

Initial codes
Document summary
User preferences
Document comments
Spell checker

In this lesson you will learn about a variety of other useful WordPerfect for Windows features. These features will save you time and make your work easier.

DEFAULT INITIAL CODES

You learned earlier that WordPerfect for Windows places codes in your document to control its formatting. If you find yourself regularly applying the same formatting to all or most of your documents, you may wish to specify *default initial codes*. Default initial codes are used automatically for all new documents that you create, saving you the trouble of manually inserting them into each new document.

Let's try it out. Suppose your usual document style uses left and right margins of 1½ inches and line spacing of 2. Here's how to specify that formatting with default initial codes. Start with a blank screen, and then:

1. Select File ➤ Preferences, and then select Initial Codes from the cascade menu. The Default Initial Codes dialog box is opened, as shown in Figure 8.1.

2. The bottom part of the screen shows the current default initial codes. The WordPerfect for Windows default initial code is [Just:Left] for left justification, as you see on the screen.

3. Enter initial formatting codes here using the usual formatting commands that you would use in a document. For margins, select Layout ➤ Margins or press Ctrl+F8, and then enter **1.5** in the Left and Right text boxes. For line spacing, select Layout ➤ Line or press Shift+F9, and then select Spacing and enter **2.**

4. When all desired codes have been entered, select Close.

FIGURE 8.1:

The Default Initial Codes dialog box

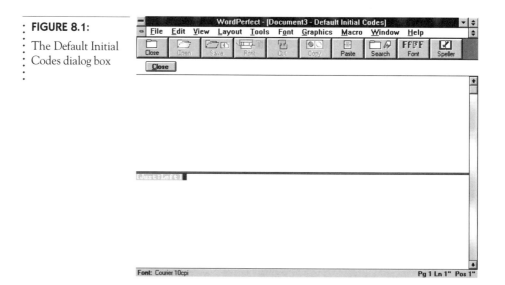

Not all formatting codes can be used as initial codes. See the Default Initial Codes entry in Part II for a list of allowed codes.

To remove an initial code, display the Default Initial Codes dialog box, move the cursor to the code, and press Del.

 The default initial codes cannot be viewed in the Reveal Codes window, but they can be modified or canceled within a document by inserting codes in the document itself.

To see the effect of the new initial codes, start typing text into the blank document on the screen. You'll see that it has the margins and line spacing you specified as initial codes. Changes you make to the Default Initial Codes affect only new documents, not the current one (unless it is blank).

 Please see the Document Initial Codes entry in Part II.

If necessary, you should clear the screen now by selecting File ➤ Close, and then answering No to the prompt.

THE DOCUMENT SUMMARY

WordPerfect for Windows gives you the option of attaching a *document summary* to each of your documents. A document summary is a short summary of important information about a document, such as its author, creation date, subject, and keywords. If you work with large numbers of documents on various subjects, proper use of document summaries can help you keep track of your work.

To see how it's done, we'll create a summary for one of our practice documents. Use the File ➤ Open command to open the practice document QUOTE. Then follow these steps (which you would also follow to view an existing summary):

1. Select Layout ➤ Document or press Ctrl+Shift+F9.

2. Select Summary. The Document Summary dialog box is displayed, as shown in Figure 8.2.

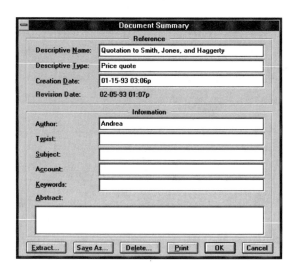

FIGURE 8.2:

The Document
Summary dialog box

3. The Creation date box lists the date the document was initially created. The Revision Date box lists the date the document was last modified. The other summary fields can be filled in with whatever information you feel is applicable; most of them are self-explanatory. For our document you should fill in the following:

- For Descriptive Name enter **Quotation to Smith, Jones, and Haggerty**
- For Descriptive Type enter **Price quote**
- For Author enter **Andrea**

4. The Summary should now appear as in Figure 8.2. Select OK or press ↵ to save the summary.

The document summary is saved as part of the current document file. The next time you open the document, you will be able to view or modify the summary.

While the Document Summary dialog box is displayed, select Print to print a copy of the summary, or select Delete to erase all of the information in the document summary.

SETTING PREFERENCES

Preferences are a variety of program settings that control the way WordPerfect for Windows functions. The initial codes that you learned about earlier in this lesson are one of the preferences you can control. You can customize WordPerfect for

Windows by making changes to the preference settings. Many preference settings are available, but most of them are beyond the scope of this book. The sections below discuss the two preference settings you are most likely to want to change.

All WordPerfect for Windows preferences have default values. If these defaults suit you, there's no need to modify any of the preferences.

BACKUP SETTINGS

The *backup* settings control when and how WordPerfect for Windows makes backup copies of your document on disk. You can specify that your document be saved automatically at regular intervals while you are working. You can also specify that an extra backup file be kept whenever you save a document.

Backup files have the same name as the original document file with a BK! extension.

The steps below show you how to set WordPerfect for Windows to automatically save your documents every ten minutes, and to keep a backup copy of each file:

1. Select File ➤ Preferences.

2. Select Backup from the cascade menu. The Backup dialog box is displayed (Figure 8.3).

FIGURE 8.3:

The Backup
dialog box

3. Select the Timed Document Backup option to have WordPerfect for Windows automatically save your document to disk periodically. In the text box enter the desired period in minutes, **10**.

4. Select the Original Document Backup option.

5. Select OK or press ↵.

LOCATION OF DOCUMENT FILES

By default, WordPerfect for Windows keeps documents in the directory where the program is installed (for example, D:\WPWIN). You may want to use another drive and/or directory as the default document location. To do so, follow these steps:

1. Select File ➤ Preferences, and then select Location of Files. The Location of Files dialog box is displayed (Figure 8.4).

2. Looking at this dialog box, you can see that there are many different types of files whose locations you can specify. Most of them you will never need to change. For now we are interested in the Documents text box. To make it current, press Alt+D.

3. Enter the full path of the new document directory. By *full path* I mean that you must enter the drive letter and the full directory tree, for example, D:\WPWIN\DOCUMENT. You can also click the file icon at the end of the text box. A dialog box will be displayed from which you can select the desired path.

4. Select OK or press ↵.

FIGURE 8.4:

The Location of Files dialog box

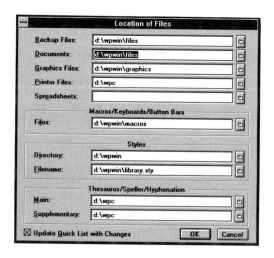

82

ADDING COMMENTS TO YOUR DOCUMENT

WordPerfect for Windows allows you to insert comments in your document during the editing process. A comment appears on the screen in a shaded box, but does not print or affect the formatting of your document. Use comments to remind yourself or others of tasks to be done, information to be added, and so on. You should still have the document QUOTE displayed on your screen; we'll add a comment to it.

1. Move the insertion point to the location for the comment. This can be anywhere in the document, even in the middle of a line. For the practice document, press Ctrl+End move to the end of the second page.

2. Select Tools ➤ Comment, and then select Create. The Create Comment dialog box is displayed (Figure 8.5).

3. Type in the text of the comment: **These figures are based on the June 5 quote we received from the manufacturer.**

4. Select OK or press ↵. The comment is displayed in the document, as shown in Figure 8.6.

When you place a comment in a document, a [Comment] code is inserted in the text. You can view this code in the Reveal Codes screen. To delete a comment, delete its code.

FIGURE 8.5:

The Create Comment dialog box

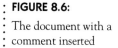

FIGURE 8.6:

The document with a comment inserted

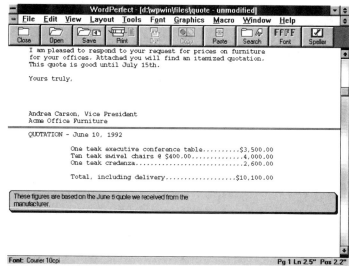

You may need to modify a comment after it has been inserted. These are the steps to follow:

1. Double-click on the comment, or move the insertion point just past the comment and select Tools ➤ Comment ➤ Edit. The Edit Comment dialog box is displayed. Except for its title, this dialog box is identical to the Create Comment dialog box shown in Figure 8.5.

2. Edit the comment as desired.

3. Select OK or press ↵.

You can display comment text in boldface, underline, and/or italics by selecting the appropriate command button at the start of the text, and then again at then end of the text. To insert a hard return in a comment, press Ctrl+↵.

You are done using this document for now. Select File ➤ Save to save it, and then select File ➤ Close to clear the screen.

USING SPECIAL CHARACTERS

A *special character* is a character or symbol that is not on your keyboard. Word-Perfect for Windows supports over 1600 special characters grouped into sets of related characters, including:

- Greek, such as θ, Σ, and Δ
- Math and scientific, such as ±, ⊆, and ∞.
- Typographic/proofreading, such as ¶, ©, and ‡.
- Symbols such as ✓, ♥ , and ♣.

WordPerfect for Windows can display these special characters on the screen and print them on just about any printer. To insert a special character, you must first select the set, and then select the character.

To see the characters in all the sets, refer to Appendix O in your WordPerfect for Windows reference manual.

Using these special characters can add polish to your documents. You should now practice inserting special characters into your document. Here are the steps to follow:

1. Select Font ➤ WP Characters or press the shortcut key, Ctrl+W.
   The WordPerfect Characters dialog box is displayed (Figure 8.7).

2. The Set pop-up box displays the name of the current character set.
   To make another set current, open the Set pop-up box and select the desired set.

3. The Characters window displays the characters in the current set. If necessary, you can scroll to view all the available characters.

4. To insert a character, you have several options:

   - Double-click the character. The dialog box remains open so you can click back and forth between the document and the dialog box to insert additional characters.
   - Click the character once, and then select Insert (to insert the character and leave the dialog box open) or Insert and Close (to insert the character and close the dialog box).

◆ Press Alt+C to make the Characters list box active. Use the arrow keys to move the dotted outline to the desired character, and then select either Insert or Insert and Close.

5. If necessary, select Close to close the dialog box.

When you next open the WordPerfect Characters dialog box, the same character set will be selected.

CHECKING YOUR SPELLING

No matter how careful you are, some misspellings and typographical errors seem to creep into most every document. WordPerfect for Windows's *speller* lets you check the spelling in your document, replacing or correcting words that are misspelled. The speller also checks for other errors such as irregular capitalization and double words.

The speller checks each word in your document against a dictionary of correct spellings. The program actually uses two dictionaries: a standard English dictionary that is supplied with the program, and a custom dictionary that you create to hold correctly spelled words that are not in the standard dictionary (such as names and technical terms).

FIGURE 8.7:

The WordPerfect Characters dialog box

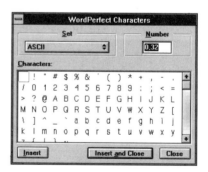

To practice using the spell checker, you should use the File ➤ Open command to open TESTMEMO, and then edit it to add the following deliberate mistakes:

- In the first line of the main text, change the *u* in *Summer* to uppercase.
- In the last sentence delete the *f* in *conflicts*.

You're now ready to start:

1. Select Tools ➤ Speller. You can also press Ctrl+F1 or click the Spell button on the Button Bar. The Speller dialog box is displayed (Figure 8.8).

2. Select Start. The Speller looks at each word in the document and compares it with the dictionary. When a word is found that is not in the dictionary, the speller highlights the word in the document and pauses. In the dialog box the Start command button changes to read Replace. In many cases the Speller will list suggested replacements for the word in the Suggestions box.

3. The speller first highlights *SUmmer* and displays the Irregular Capitalization dialog box. You should select Replace; the text will be corrected to *Summer*. You could also select Continue (to go on without making the correction) or Disable Checking (to turn off case checking).

4. The speller next highlights *conlicts*. Several suggestions are displayed in the Suggestions list box, with the correct spelling *conflicts* highlighted. Select Replace to replace the highlighted word in the document with the highlighted word in the Suggestions list box. To highlight a different word in the Suggestions list, click it or use the arrow keys. If you do not want to replace the highlighted word with one of the words in the Suggestions dialog box, you have several options:

- Select Add if the word is not actually misspelled (your name, for example) and you want to add it to the dictionary.
- Select Skip Once to skip this instance of the word but flag future instances in the document.
- Select Skip Always to skip this and all future instances of the word in the document.
- To edit the highlighted word in the document, click it and edit as usual. When you do this, the Replace button in the dialog box changes to Resume. When you're finished editing the word, select Resume to continue with the spelling check.
- Select Close if you want to terminate the spell check operation before it is finished.

5. When the spelling check is complete, a message to that effect is displayed. Select OK or press ↵.

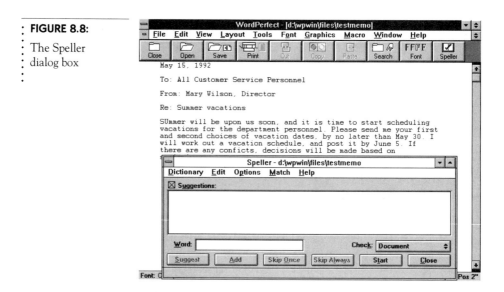

In the Speller dialog box, the Check pop-up box offers several options. The default is Document, which means that the entire document will be checked. The other options available are:

- ◆ Word: checks the spelling of the word the insertion point is on.
- ◆ To End of Document: checks from the insertion point to the end of the document.
- ◆ Page: checks the current page.
- ◆ To End of Page: checks from the insertion point to the end of the current page.
- ◆ Selected Text: checks the selected text.
- ◆ To End of Selection: checks from the insertion point to the end of the selected text.

The last two options are available only if you select text before displaying the Speller dialog box.

In addition to misspelled words, the Speller will optionally flag words that contain numbers (for example, "th4"), and duplicate words (for example, " Our annual profit profit was…"). All three of these options are on by default. To turn them off, display the Options menu in the Speller dialog box, and then select the desired option.

SUMMARY

This lesson covered a variety of useful WordPerfect for Windows features. You learned how to set the default initial codes to apply certain formatting to all your new documents automatically. You saw how to control where WordPerfect for Windows looks for document files, and how and when it makes backups. You also learned how to insert nonprinting comments in a document, and how to use special characters. Finally you saw how to use WordPerfect for Windows's spell checker to verify the spelling in your document.

You should save your document now, but leave it on screen. We'll be using it in the next lesson.

FOR MORE INFORMATION

You will find additional information about the topics covered in this lesson by consulting the following reference entries in Part II:

Comments

Default Initial Codes

Document Initial Codes

Document Summary

Special Characters

Speller

LESSON 9

WORKING WITH MULTIPLE DOCUMENTS

INTRODUCING

Viewing two or more documents

Copying text between documents

Closing documents

One of the most powerful features in Word-Perfect for Windows is that it allows you to work on multiple documents at the same time. You can have as many as nine different documents open at once. Few people ever need this many, but it often can be handy to have two or three open.

If you're not continuing from the previous lesson, you should open the file TESTMEMO now.

OPENING A SECOND DOCUMENT

While you are working on one document, you can open another document. The second document can be a totally new document, or can be an existing document on disk. Opening a new document has no effect on the original document.

With TESTMEMO open, follow these steps to open a second document:

1. Select File ➤ Open, press F4, or click the Open button on the Button Bar. The Open File dialog box is displayed. This is the same Open File dialog box you learned about in Lesson 2.

2. Type in the name of the file to open, or select it from the Files list box. You should select QUOTE. Then, press ↵ or select OK.

3. The file is opened and displayed on the screen. The original document TESTMEMO is temporarily hidden.

To open a new, blank document, select File ➤ New or press Shift+F4. A blank editing window is opened and given the temporary name DOCUMENTn, where n is a digit 1–9.

VIEWING MULTIPLE DOCUMENTS

When you have multiple documents open, they are all in WordPerfect for Windows's memory and available for editing, printing, and so on. Each individual document is kept in its own window. You can have a single window displayed full-screen, with the others hidden. Or, as you'll learn soon, you can have two or more document windows displayed at the same time, each taking up a portion of the screen. In either case, only one document window is *active*. The active document contains the insertion point, and it is the only document affected by commands you issue. You can switch between document windows, making each one active as you need to work on it.

The status bar displays information about the active document.

SWITCHING BETWEEN FULL-SCREEN DOCUMENTS

The WordPerfect for Windows default is to display each document in a full-screen window, which means that you can view only one document (the active one) at a time. To switch between documents you have two choices:

- Press Ctrl+F6 one or more times to cycle through the open documents. Each press makes the next document active and displays it on the screen. You can also press Ctrl+Shift+F6 to cycle backward through the open documents.

- Select Window. The Window menu displays a list of all open documents, with a checkmark next to the currently active one (Figure 9.1). Use the usual menu selection methods to select the desired document.

    Go ahead and try it: press Ctrl+F6 once and TESTMEMO is displayed; press Ctrl+F6 again and QUOTE is displayed. You should also try using the Window menu to switch between documents.

DISPLAYING MULTIPLE DOCUMENTS AT ONE TIME

At times you may want to have two or more documents displayed at the same time. For example, you might want to refer to text in one document while typing in another. When you display multiple documents, each one is in its own window.

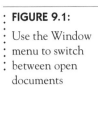

FIGURE 9.1:

Use the Window menu to switch between open documents

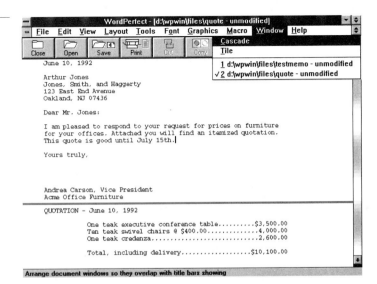

The title bar of each window displays the filename of the document it contains. You can arrange the windows on the screen in two ways:

- Select Window ➤ Cascade for *cascaded* windows. Cascaded windows are displayed in a partially overlapping stack, much as you might hold playing cards in your hand. The active document window is on top and is fully visible. Only the title bars of inactive windows are visible. Figure 9.2 shows cascaded windows.

- Select Window ➤ Tile for *tiled* windows. Tiled windows do not overlap. Each window occupies an equal fraction of the screen area. Figure 9.3 shows tiled widows.

Try both of these commands now. Remember that only one window is active at a time. The active window's title bar is highlighted, and it displays a vertical scroll bar at the right edge. In addition, only the active window displays the *Control menu box* (the small box at the left end of the title bar) and the *sizing buttons* (the small boxes at the right end of the title bar). In Figures 9.2 and 9.3 the QUOTE window is active. You'll learn about the Control menu box and sizing buttons soon.

Use cascaded windows when you want to see what documents you have open. Use tiled windows when you need to view the contents of those documents.

When windows are tiled or cascaded, you can switch the active window with Ctrl+F6 or Ctrl+Shift+F6, or with the Window menu, as described above. You can

FIGURE 9.2:

Cascaded windows overlap, with the active document on top

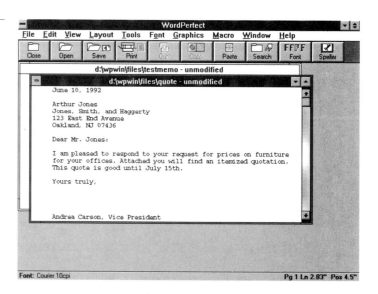

FIGURE 9.3:

Tiled document
windows do not
overlap

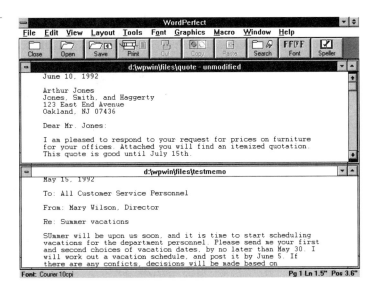

also make any visible window active by clicking anywhere in the window or on its title bar.

CONTROLLING WINDOW SIZE AND POSITION

When a window is displayed less than full-screen size, you can modify its size to suit your editing needs and make it full-screen size or any other size you want. To change the size, you use the *Control menu*.

Every WordPerfect for Windows window has a Control menu. The Control menu for the active document window can be displayed in three ways:

- ◆ Press Alt+− (Alt plus the minus key).
- ◆ Click the Control menu box. As you learned above, the Control menu box is at the left end of a window's title bar or, if the window is at full-screen size, at the left end of the menu bar.
- ◆ Press F10 followed by ↵ or ↓.

Figure 9.4 shows a document window with its Control menu opened. Once the Control menu is displayed, you access its commands just like any other menu. You'll learn about these commands soon.

You should note that the WordPerfect for Windows program itself has its own Control menu box and sizing buttons that are displayed, respectively, in the upper-left and upper-right corners of the screen. These are used to control the Word-Perfect for Windows program, and are distinct from the document window Control menu box and sizing buttons. For further information, please refer to your Microsoft Windows documentation.

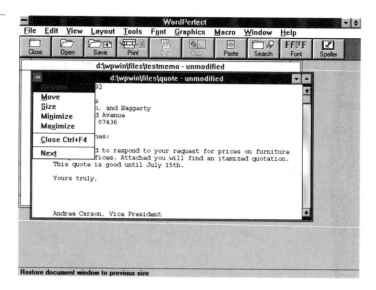

FIGURE 9.4:

Each document window has its own Control menu

To return a small window to full-screen size, display the Control menu and select Maximize, or click the sizing button that has the up-pointing triangle. Try this now with one of your document windows.

When a window is displayed full-screen, it has only a single sizing button that contains up- and down-pointing triangles. This is called the restore button.

To return a full-screen window to its previous smaller size, display the Control menu and select Restore, or click the restore button. Do this now with your full-screen document window.

When a window is displayed at less than full-screen size, you can resize it to any desired dimensions. To resize a window with the keyboard:

1. Display the Control menu.

2. Select Size.

3. Use the arrow keys to stretch or shrink the window outline to the desired size.

4. Press ↵

To resize a window with the mouse, point at an edge or corner of the window. The pointer will change to a double-headed arrow. Then, drag the window outline to the desired size.

A window can be moved only when it is displayed at less than full-screen size. To move a window with the keyboard:

1. Display the Control menu.

2. Select Move.

3. Use the arrow keys to move the window outline to the desired position.

4. Press ↵.

To move a window with the mouse, point at the window's title bar and drag the window outline to the desired position.

You should spend a little time using these methods to change the size and positions of your two document windows. By controlling both size and position, you can arrange multiple documents just about any way you like.

TIP *All of the commands on the Control menu can be executed more quickly using the mouse.*

COPYING AND MOVING TEXT BETWEEN DOCUMENTS

One of the most important ways you'll use the WordPerfect for Windows multiple document capabilities is to copy and move text from one document to another. Suppose that you need to write a promotional letter to a prospective customer. You remember a successful letter that you wrote to another customer several months ago. You would open two document windows, a blank one for the new letter and another for the existing letter. Then, by copying phrases from the old to the new, you could finish your letter in much less time than it would take to write it from scratch.

The basic procedure for copying or moving text between documents is as follows:

1. Make the window containing the source document active.

2. Select the text you want to copy or move. Remember that you can copy/move formatting codes as well as text.

3. To copy, select Edit ➤ Copy, press Ctrl+Ins, or click the Copy button on the Button Bar. To move, select Edit ➤ Cut, press Shift+Del, or click the Cut button on the Button Bar.

4. Make the window containing the destination document active.

5. Move the insertion point to the location where you want the text.

6. Select Edit ➤ Paste, press Shift+Ins, or click the Paste button on the Button Bar.

Try this now. Imagine that you need to write a new memo, and you would like to copy the applicable text from TESTMEMO into the new memo. You should already have TESTMEMO open. Then:

1. Select File ➤ New to open a blank document window.

2. Press Ctrl+F6 one or more times to make TESTMEMO active.

3. Select text in TESTMEMO from the beginning of the document up to the colon in *Re:*.

4. Press Ctrl+Ins.

5. Press Ctrl+F6 one or more times to make the blank document window active.

6. Press Shift+Ins. The text is inserted into the new document.

SAVING MULTIPLE DOCUMENTS

When you have multiple documents open, saving them is no different from saving a single document. You must save them individually, using the File ➤ Save or File ➤ Save As commands. These commands save only the document in the active window. To save all open documents, you must make each one active in turn and save it.

CLOSING DOCUMENT WINDOWS

When you are working with multiple documents, it's a good idea to close each document when you are finished with it. To close a document:

1. Make the document window active.

2. Select File ➤ Close or press Ctrl+F4.

3. If the document has been changed since the last time it was saved, a dialog box is displayed asking if you want to save the changes.

4. Select Yes to save the changes and close the document. Select No to close the document without saving the changes.

5. The document window is closed. If another document is open, its window becomes active. If no other document is open, a new, blank document window is displayed.

In turn, you should now make each of your open documents active and save it.

SUMMARY

This lesson has introduced you to the WordPerfect for Windows multiple document capabilities. You learned how to open multiple documents, each in its own window. You also learned how to select the active window, and how to control the size and position of windows.

Congratulations! You have completed the tutorial portion of this book. You now know enough about WordPerfect for Windows to start using it for real-world tasks. If you need occasional reminders about how to do something, or if you want information about the program's more advanced features, you can refer to the reference entries in Part II.

FOR MORE INFORMATION

You will find additional information about the topics covered in this lesson by consulting the following reference entries in Part II:

Closing a Document

Opening a File

PART TWO

Reference

A

APPENDING TEXT

PURPOSE To copy selected text to the clipboard, adding it to the end of whatever is already on the clipboard.

TO APPEND TEXT TO THE CLIPBOARD

1. Select the text.
2. Select Edit ➤ Append.

NOTES Edit ➤ Append works like Edit ➤ Copy does, except that the selected text is appended to the existing clipboard contents, rather than replacing it. Use Append to gather sections of text from various document locations onto the clipboard, and then use Edit ➤ Paste to insert the clipboard contents into a document.

See Also Copying Text, Moving Text

AUTO CODE PLACEMENT

PURPOSE To control the location of formatting codes that affect entire paragraphs or pages.

TO TURN AUTO CODE PLACEMENT ON OR OFF

1. Select File ➤ Preferences ➤ Environment.
2. In the Settings section of the dialog box, select the Auto Code Placement option.
3. Select OK or press ↵.

NOTES Certain WordPerfect for Windows formatting codes normally affect entire paragraphs or pages. If Auto Code Placement is on (the default), these codes will be placed at the beginning of the current paragraph or page (depending on the code) no matter where the insertion point is positioned. If this option is off, the codes will be placed at the insertion point position. For most purposes Auto Code Placement should be left on.

AUTOMATIC BACKUP

PURPOSE To control when WordPerfect for Windows makes backup copies of your documents.

TO SET BACKUP OPTIONS

1. Select File ➤ Preferences ➤ Backup. The Backup dialog box is displayed.

2. Select Timed Document Backup to have WordPerfect for Windows automatically save your document to disk periodically. In the text box enter the desired period, in minutes, between backups.

3. Select Original Document Backup to have WordPerfect for Windows keep a backup of the previous version of your document each time it is saved.

NOTES When Timed Document Backup is turned on, WordPerfect for Windows will periodically save your document to disk (just as if you had selected the File ➤ Save command).

When Original Document Backup is on, WordPerfect for Windows will make a backup of the previous version of your document each time it is saved. The backup file will have the original document filename with the BK! extension and will contain the document as it was the last time you saved it.

BLOCK PROTECT

PURPOSE To prevent a block of text from being split between two pages.

TO PROTECT A BLOCK

1. Select the text to be kept on one page.
2. Select Layout ➤ Page or press Alt+F9.
3. Select Block Protect.

NOTES The text to be protected must be less than a page in length. If the normal document formatting would result in the block being split between two pages, a soft page break is inserted just before the block. If you have consecutive protected blocks, they must be separated by at least one soft or hard return.

See Also Conditional End of Page, Widow/Orphan Protection

BOLD

TO BOLD EXISTING TEXT

1. Select the text.
2. Select Font ➤ Bold or press Ctrl+B.

TO BOLD AS YOU TYPE

1. Select Font ➤ Bold or press Ctrl+B to begin bold.
2. Type in the text.
3. Select Font ➤ Bold or press Ctrl+B again to end bold.

NOTES Boldface can be combined with italics, underlining, and other font attributes.

See Also Selecting Text

BUTTON BAR

PURPOSE To provide quick mouse access to commonly needed program commands. You can hide or display the Button Bar by selecting View ➤ Button Bar. You can also create customized Button Bars.

TO CREATE A NEW USER-DEFINED BUTTON BAR

1. Select View ➤ Button Bar Setup ➤ New.

2. A blank Button Bar is displayed along with the Edit Button Bar dialog box. Use the mouse and the following techniques to design your Button Bar:

- ◆ To add a command to the Button Bar, select the command from the menus.

- ◆ To add a macro to the Button Bar, select Assign Macro to Button, select the desired macro, and then select Assign.

- ◆ To remove a command or macro from the Button Bar, drag the button off the bar.

- ◆ To move a command or macro to a different position on the bar, drag the button to the new location.

3. When the Button Bar is complete, select OK.

4. Enter a name for the Button Bar, and then select Save.

TO MODIFY THE CURRENT BUTTON BAR

1. Select View ➤ Button Bar Setup ➤ Edit.

2. The Edit Button Bar dialog box is displayed. Use the mouse and the following techniques to edit your Button Bar:

- ◆ To add a new command to the Button Bar, select the command from the menus.

- ◆ To add a macro to the Button Bar, select Assign Macro to Button, select the desired macro, and then select Assign.

- ◆ To remove a command or macro from the Button Bar, drag the button off the bar.

- ◆ To move a command or macro to a different position on the bar, drag the button to the new location.

3. When you are finished editing the Button Bar, select OK.

TO SELECT WHICH BUTTON BAR IS DISPLAYED ON-SCREEN

1. Select View ➤ Button Bar Setup ➤ Select.

2. The Select Button Bar dialog box is displayed. Select the desired Button Bar.

3. Press ↵ or click Select.

NOTES If a Button Bar has more buttons than can be displayed at once, arrows are added to let you scroll left and right on the Button Bar. WordPerfect for Windows has several specialized Button Bars. The default Button Bar is called WP{WP}.WWB. The TABLES.WWB Button Bar is designed for manipulating tables; you can select this Button Bar as described above. Other specialized Button Bars are displayed automatically on the Print Preview screen and the Equation Editor screen.

CASE CONVERSIONS

PURPOSE To change letters between upper- and lowercase.

TO CHANGE THE CASE OF LETTERS

1. Select the text to be changed.
2. Select Edit ➤ Convert Case, and then select either Uppercase or Lowercase.
3. All letters in the selected text change to the specified case.

NOTES When you convert to lowercase, the following words remain capitalized:

- The word *I*.
- Words starting with *I* followed by an apostrophe, such as *I'm* and *I'll*.
- The first word in a sentence (but only if the punctuation that ends the preceding sentence is included in the text selection).

CENTER PAGE

PURPOSE To center text top-to-bottom on a page.

TO CENTER A PAGE VERTICALLY

1. Type the text you want centered on a page.
2. Insert hard page breaks at the beginning and end of the text. If it's the first page in the document, you need to insert a hard page break only at the end of the text.
3. Press Alt+Home to move the cursor to the start of the page.
4. Select Layout ➤ Page or press Alt+F9.
5. Select Center Page.

NOTES Centering a page vertically works only if the page contains fewer lines than the normal "full page" amount. To avoid problems with automatic page breaks, separate the page from the previous and next pages by hard page breaks. Page centering is not visible during normal editing but can be seen on the Print Preview screen.

See Also Margins

CENTERING TEXT

See Justification

CHARACTERS

See Special Characters

CLIPBOARD OPERATIONS

See Appending Text, Copying Text, Moving Text

CLOSING A DOCUMENT

PURPOSE To close the active window and optionally save changes to the document it contains.

TO CLOSE A DOCUMENT

1. Select File ➤ Close or click the Close button.
2. If the document has been modified since the last time it was saved, you are asked whether the changes should be saved.
3. Select Yes to save the changes and close the document. Select No to discard the changes and close the document. Select Cancel to return to editing the document.

CODES

See Formatting Codes

COLUMNS

PURPOSE To display text in either newspaper columns or parallel columns. Using columns is a two-stage process: you must first define the type and number of columns you want, and then turn columns on and off as you need them in your document.

TO DEFINE COLUMNS

1. Move the insertion point to the location where you want columns to begin.

2. Select Layout ➤ Columns or press Alt+Shift+F9, and then select Define. The Define Columns dialog box is displayed.

3. In the Number of Columns text box enter the desired number of columns.

4. Under Type specify the type of columns to be created (see the Notes section below).

5. If the Evenly Spaced option is selected, WordPerfect for Windows will automatically enter margin settings for evenly spaced columns in the Margins section. You can change these settings if desired.

6. To change the width of the gutter space between evenly spaced columns, enter the new value in the Distance Between Columns text box.

7. To define the columns and begin them in your document, select the Columns On checkbox. To define columns without beginning them, turn the Columns On checkbox off.

8. Select OK or press ↵.

TO TURN COLUMNS ON OR OFF

1. Select Layout ➤ Columns or press Alt+Shift+F9.

2. Select Columns On or Columns Off.

TO CONVERT EXISTING TEXT TO COLUMNS

1. Define the columns as described above, with the insertion point located before the text. If the document already contains a column definition, you can omit this step.

2. Move the insertion point to the start of the text to be converted to columns.

3. Select Layout ➤ Columns ➤ Columns On.

4. Move the insertion point to the end of the text that you want in columns.

5. Select Layout ➤ Columns ➤ Columns Off.

TO CONVERT COLUMNS TO REGULAR TEXT

1. Select View ➤ Reveal Codes or press Alt+F3 to display formatting codes.

2. To return a single set of columns to normal text, delete the [Col On] code at the start of the columns. To return all columns in the document to normal text, delete the [Col Def:] code.

TO ENTER TEXT IN COLUMNS

1. Type in the text in the usual fashion. It will be automatically formatted to fit within the defined columns.

2. To move to the next column, press Ctrl+↵. If you are in the last column, pressing Ctrl+↵ moves the insertion point to the first column on the next page.

TO MOVE AROUND IN COLUMNS

1. Within a column, movement keys function normally. Thus, pressing End moves the insertion point to the end of the current line within the current column.

2. To move from one column to another, click in the destination column. You can also select Edit ➤ Go To or press Ctrl+G to display the Go To dialog box, and then select the desired destination from the Position pop-up list. When the insertion point is in a column, this list contains column-related destinations (for example, Next Column, First Column).

NOTES There are three types of columns available. In *newspaper columns* text flows from the bottom of one column to the top of the next column, as in newspapers and brochures. In *parallel columns* related text is placed side by side, as in scripts and lists. *Parallel columns with block protect* are identical to parallel columns except that each row of text is kept on the same page.

You can create between two and twenty-four columns on a page. Unless you specify otherwise, the columns will be of equal width. When you turn columns on, the document will have the columns described in the previous column definition code. When you turn columns off, the rest of the document reverts to normal text.

If the ruler is displayed, you can click the Columns button to create two to five evenly spaced newspaper style columns, and to turn columns on and off. If you double-click the Columns button, the Define Columns dialog box is displayed.

It is often easier to do most of your document editing with columns off. Then, as the document nears completion, turn columns on for final editing.

See Also Default Initial Codes, Ruler, Tables

COMMENTS

PURPOSE To insert a nonprinting comment in a document.

TO INSERT A COMMENT

1. Move the insertion point to the location for the comment.
2. Select Tools ➤ Comment, and then select Create. The Create Comment dialog box is displayed.
3. Type in the text of the comment. You can display text in the comment in boldface, underline, and/or italics by selecting the appropriate command button at the start of the text, and then again at the end of the text. To insert a hard return in a comment, press Ctrl+↵.
4. Select OK or press ↵. The comment is displayed in the document.

TO EDIT AN EXISTING COMMENT

1. Double-click on the comment, or move the insertion point just past the comment and select Tools ➤ Comment ➤ Edit. The Edit Comment dialog box is displayed.
2. Edit the comment as desired.
3. Select OK or press ↵.

TO CONVERT TEXT INTO A COMMENT

1. Select the text to be converted into a comment.
2. Select Tools ➤ Comment ➤ Create.

TO CONVERT A COMMENT INTO DOCUMENT TEXT

1. Move the insertion point to a position just below the comment.
2. Select Tools ➤ Comment ➤ Convert to Text.

NOTES A comment appears on the screen in a shaded box but does not print or affect the format of your document.

Comments do not display in portions of the document where columns are turned on. The Comment code remains in the text and will display if columns are turned off.

COMPARE DOCUMENTS

PURPOSE To compare the current document with one on disk and mark the differences between them.

TO COMPARE THE CURRENT DOCUMENT WITH ONE ON DISK

1. Select Tools ➤ Document Compare ➤ Add Markings. The Add Markings dialog box is displayed.

2. The File to Compare text box contains the name of the current document. If you want to compare the current version of this document (which you have edited) with the previous version on disk, select Add Markings or press ↵. To compare with a different disk document, enter its name, and then select Add Markings or press ↵.

3. The differences between the documents are marked and the insertion point is moved to the start of the document.

TO REMOVE MARKINGS

1. To remove all comparison markings, returning the document to its state before the comparison, select Edit ➤ Undo immediately after performing the comparison.

or

1. Select Tools ➤ Document Compare ➤ Remove Markings. The Remove Markings dialog box is displayed.

2. To remove all markings, select OK or press ↵. To retain added phrases and remove other markings, select Leave Redline Marks, and then select OK or press ↵.

NOTES WordPerfect starts at the beginning of the document and compares text on a phrase-by-phrase basis. A *phrase* is text between any two of the following: punctuation, Hard Return code, Hard Page code, Footnote/Endnote codes, and end of document. Differences are marked as follows:

- A phrase present in the current document but not in the disk document is marked with a pair of redline codes [Redln On][Redln Off]. The phrase is displayed in red on color monitors or in reverse video on monochrome monitors.

- A phrase present in the disk document but not in the current document is marked with a pair of strikeout codes [Stkout On][Stkout Off]. The phrase is displayed with a line drawn through it.

- A phrase that has been moved has *THE FOLLOWING TEXT WAS MOVED* placed before it and *THE PRECEDING TEXT WAS MOVED* placed after it.

The document comparison includes text in footnotes, endnotes, and tables. It does not include text in graphics boxes, headers, and footers.

See Also Redline/Strikeout

CONDITIONAL END OF PAGE

PURPOSE To keep a specified number of lines together on one page.

TO SPECIFY A CONDITIONAL END OF PAGE

1. Move the insertion point to the line just above the lines to be kept together.
2. Select Layout ➤ Page or press Alt+F9.
3. Select Conditional End of Page.
4. Enter the number of lines to be kept together.
5. Select OK or press ↵.

NOTES The number of lines that you specify in step 4 must include any blank lines resulting from double- or triple-spaced text.

See Also Block Protect, Widow/Orphan Protection

COPYING TEXT

TO COPY TEXT

1. Select the text and/or codes to be copied.
2. Select Edit ➤ Copy, press Ctrl+Ins, or click the Copy button on the Button Bar.
3. Move the insertion point to the destination location.
4. Select Edit ➤ Paste, press Shift+Ins, or click the Paste button on the Button Bar.

See Also Moving Text, Selecting Text

CROSS REFERENCE

PURPOSE To refer to another part of the document by page number. A cross reference consists of two parts. The *reference* is where you refer readers to another part of the document. The *target* is the location the reader is told to look. The target can be a variety of items, including a page number, a figure number, or a footnote number. A document can have an unlimited number of cross references. Each reference is tied to its target by a unique *target name*. After references and targets are specified, you must then generate the cross references so WordPerfect for Windows can determine and insert the correct numbers.

TO MARK A REFERENCE

1. Move the insertion point to the location where you want the cross reference.

2. Type any introductory text (such as *Please refer to page*) followed by a space.

3. Select Tools ➤ Mark Text or press F12, and then select Cross Reference. The Mark Cross Reference dialog box is displayed.

4. Select the Reference option.

5. Open the Tie Reference To pop-up list and select the type of target that the reference will be tied to.

6. In the Target Name box enter the name of the target that this reference will be tied to.

7. Select OK or press ↵.

TO MARK A TARGET

1. Move the insertion point just past the target.

2. Select Tools ➤ Mark Text or press F12, and then select Cross Reference. The Mark Cross Reference dialog box is displayed.

3. Select the Target option.

4. In the Target Name box enter the name to be used to refer to this target.

5. Select OK or press ↵.

TO MARK A REFERENCE AND TARGET IN ONE OPERATION

1. Move the insertion point to the location where you want the cross reference.
2. Type any introductory text (such as *Please refer to page*) followed by a space.
3. Select Tools ➤ Mark Text or press F12, and then select Cross Reference. The Mark Cross Reference dialog box is displayed.
4. Select the Reference and Target option.
5. Open the Tie Reference To pop-up list and select the type of target that the reference will be tied.
6. In the Target Name box enter a target name.
7. Select OK or press ↵. A message instructs you to move to the target.
8. Move the insertion point just past the target, and then press ↵.

TO GENERATE CROSS REFERENCES

1. Select Tools ➤ Generate or press Alt+F12.
2. Select Yes. All cross references in the document, as well as other addenda (index, table of contents, and lists) will be generated.

NOTES The target name is not displayed or printed, but serves only to tie a reference to its target. You can create multiple references to one target. To have a single reference refer to multiple targets (for example, *Please see pages 3, 5, 8*), create multiple targets with the same name.

See Also Index, Lists, Table of Contents

CUTTING AND PASTING

See Moving Text

DATE

PURPOSE To insert the current date or a date code into a document.

TO INSERT THE DATE

- To insert today's date as text, select Tools ➤ Date ➤ Text or press Ctrl+F5.
- To insert a code that always displays as the current date, select Tools ➤ Date ➤ Code or press Ctrl+Shift+F5.
- To specify the format used for dates, select Tools ➤ Date ➤ Format.

NOTES A date code in a document will always display as the date set on your computer's system clock.

DEFAULT INITIAL CODES

PURPOSE To control the default formatting for all new documents.

TO SPECIFY DEFAULT INITIAL CODES

1. Select File ➤ Preferences ➤ Initial Codes. The Default Initial Codes dialog box is opened.
2. The bottom part of the screen shows the current initial codes. The Word-Perfect for Windows default initial code is [Just:Left] for left justification, so it is already on the screen.
3. Enter formatting codes here using the usual commands. To remove codes, move the cursor to them and press Del. You cannot enter text on this screen.
4. When all desired codes have been entered, select Close.

NOTES Changes you make to the Default Initial Codes affect only new documents, not the current one. Initial codes cannot be viewed in the Reveal Codes window, but they can be overridden by document initial codes and by codes inserted in a document during editing. Only the following codes can be used as initial codes:

Column Definition

Column On

Decimal/Align Character

Endnote Number

Endnote Options

Font

Footnote Number

Footnote Options

Graphics Box Number

Graphics Box Options

Hyphenation On/Off

Hyphenation Zone

Justification

Kerning

Language

Letter Spacing

Line Height

Line Numbering

Line Spacing

Margins

New Page Number

Page Numbering Style

Paper Size

Suppress Page Format

Tab Set

Text Color

Underline Spaces and Tabs

Widow/Orphan On/Off

Word Spacing

D

See Also Document Initial Codes

DELETING TEXT

TO DELETE TEXT

To delete a block of text, first select the text, and then press Del or Backspace. You can also delete text as follows:

- ◆ Press Backspace to delete one character to the left of the insertion point.
- ◆ Press Del to delete one character to the right of the insertion point.
- ◆ Press Ctrl+Backspace to delete the word at the insertion point.
- ◆ Press Ctrl+Del to delete from the insertion point to the end of the line.

See Also Undeleting Text

DISPLAY OPTIONS

PURPOSE To control the way your document is displayed.

TO SET DISPLAY OPTIONS

1. Select View. On the pull-down menu are three display options:

   - ◆ When Draft Mode is on, all text is displayed in the same monospaced font and graphic images are hidden. Font and attribute changes are indicated by colors.
   - ◆ When Graphics is on, graphics images are displayed during editing. When this option is off, graphics images are displayed as empty boxes.
   - ◆ When Comments is on, document comments are displayed. When this option is off, comments are hidden.

2. Select an option to turn it on or off. A check is displayed next to an option when it is active.

NOTES Select Draft Mode for faster editing and screen display in a document that contains many different fonts. Turn Graphics off for faster response when editing text in a document that contains a lot of graphics images.

See Also Comments

DOCUMENT INITIAL CODES

PURPOSE To control the default formatting for the current document.

TO SPECIFY DOCUMENT INITIAL CODES

1. Select Layout ➤ Document or press Ctrl+Shift+F9, and then select Initial Codes. The Document Initial Codes dialog box is opened.
2. The bottom part of the screen shows the current document initial codes, if any.
3. Enter formatting codes here using the usual commands. To remove codes, move the cursor to them and press Del.
4. When all desired codes have been entered, select Close.

NOTES You cannot enter text on the Initial Codes screen. A document's initial codes cannot be viewed in the Reveal Codes window, but they can be modified or canceled within a document by inserting codes in the document itself. Document initial codes override any default initial codes that have been set. Only certain codes can be used as initial codes; see the Default Initial Codes entry for a list of allowed codes.

See Also Default Initial Codes, Formatting Codes

DOCUMENT SUMMARY

PURPOSE To summarize important information about a document for reference purposes.

TO ENTER INFORMATION IN THE DOCUMENT SUMMARY

1. Select Layout ➤ Document or press Ctrl+Shift+F9.
2. Select Summary. The Document Summary dialog box is displayed.
3. The Creation Date field lists the date the document was initially created. The Revision Date field lists the date the document was last modified.
4. Fill in the other summary fields as desired.
5. The Abstract field provides space to enter a longer description of the contents of the document. It can be many lines long. If you want to insert a hard return in the abstract, press Ctrl+↵.
6. Select OK or press ↵ to save the summary.

NOTES While the Document Summary dialog box is displayed, you can select Print to print the summary, or select Delete to clear all summary fields.

DOUBLE UNDERLINE

TO DOUBLE-UNDERLINE EXISTING TEXT

1. Select the text.
2. Select Font ➤ Double Underline.

TO DOUBLE-UNDERLINE AS YOU TYPE

1. Select Font ➤ Double Underline to begin underlining.
2. Type in the text.
3. Select Font ➤ Double Underline to end underlining.

NOTES Double underlining can be combined with bold, italics, and other font attributes.

See Also Selecting Text, Underline

ENDNOTES

PURPOSE To add notes to the end of the document rather than at the bottom of each page, as footnotes are. WordPerfect for Windows will automatically number endnotes.

TO CREATE AN ENDNOTE

1. Move the insertion point to the location in the document where you want the number for the endnote inserted.
2. Select Layout ➤ Endnote ➤ Create. The Endnote window is opened with the number of the new endnote displayed.
3. Type in the endnote text. You can use most of the WordPerfect for Window formatting and editing commands in an endnote.
4. When the endnote is finished, select Close.
5. The endnote number is displayed in the document, but the endnote itself is displayed only on the Print Preview screen.

TO EDIT AN ENDNOTE

1. Select Layout ➤ Endnote ➤ Edit. The Edit Endnote dialog box is displayed.
2. Enter the number of the note you want to edit and press ↵. The Endnote screen is opened with the selected endnote displayed for editing.
3. Make the desired changes, and then select Close.

TO CHANGE ENDNOTE LOCATION

Endnotes are printed at the end of the document by default. You can print them, however, at one or more other locations in the document. For example, you can print them at the ends of subdocument chapters in a book-length master document.

1. Move the insertion point to the desired endnote location.
2. Select Layout ➤ Endnote ➤ Placement. The Endnote Placement dialog box is displayed.
3. Select Yes to restart endnote numbering. Select No if you do not want to restart endnote numbering.

E

4. An Endnote Placement code is inserted in the document, followed by a Hard Page Break. In addition, a nonprinting comment is inserted to mark the endnote placement location.

5. When the document is printed, all endnotes from the beginning of the document (or the previous Endnote Placement code) are printed at the location of the Endnote Placement code.

TO MODIFY ENDNOTE OPTIONS

1. Select Layout ➤ Endnote ➤ Options. The Endnote Options dialog box is displayed.

2. Open the Numbering Method pop-up list and select the numbering method. Select Numbers (the default) for sequential numbers. Select Letters for sequential letters (a, b, c, and so on). Select Characters to use the character you enter in the Characters text box. The character will be used by itself for the first endnote, then doubled, and so on (*, **, ***, etc.).

3. The Style in Text box specifies how the endnote number appears in the body of the document. The Style in Note box specifies how the number appears in the endnote. In both, the [Note Num] code represents the number itself. To enter codes in these boxes, open the pop-up list for each one.

4. The Line Spacing in Notes setting controls the spacing of lines within notes. The Spacing Between Notes setting controls the amount of blank space inserted between consecutive notes.

5. When all options are set as you want them, select OK or press ↵.

TO CHANGE ENDNOTE NUMBERING

1. Move the insertion point to where you want the new endnote numbering to start.

2. Select Layout ➤ Endnote ➤ New Number. The New Number dialog box is displayed.

3. Enter the new endnote number, and then select OK or press ↵.

NOTES When you add or delete an endnote, other endnotes are automatically renumbered as needed to maintain sequential endnote numbering throughout the document.

To delete an endnote, use the Reveal Codes window to find the Endnote code, and delete it.

See Also Comments, Default Initial Codes, Footnotes, Headers and Footers, Master Documents, Print Preview

EQUATION EDITOR

PURPOSE To create mathematical and scientific equations in your documents. Please note that the Equation Editor displays and prints equations—it does not solve them. It is very powerful, offering a full range of mathematical symbols and commands for manipulating them. With this power comes complexity. A detailed explanation of how the Equation Editor works is beyond the scope of this book. Essentially, you create and edit equations by typing numbers, variables, and standard keyboard symbols in an editing window; selecting commands that insert and align special symbols from an equation palette; and checking a graphical view of your work in a display window. Please see your WordPerfect for Windows documentation for further information.

See Also Graphics Boxes

EXPORTING FILES

PURPOSE To save a document in a format that can be used by another program.

TO EXPORT A FILE

1. Select File ➤ Save As. The Save As dialog box is displayed.
2. In the Save As text box enter a name for the exported file.
3. Open the Format pop-up list and select the name of the program whose format you want to use.
4. Select Save or press ↵.

See Also Importing Files

FIGURE EDITOR

PURPOSE To edit graphic images in a document. For information on inserting graphics images in a document, please see the Graphics Boxes entry.

TO DISPLAY AN IMAGE FOR EDITING

1. Select Graphics ➤ Figure ➤ Edit, and then enter the number of the box to edit.

2. With the mouse, double-click the box you want to edit.

TO MODIFY AN IMAGE

When you edit an image, you cannot actually change the contents of the image, adding new elements or deleting existing elements. You can only modify the way the image is displayed—its colors, size, rotation, and so on. The editing commands are found on the Edit menu; most of them are on the Button Bar as well.

Move	Changes the image's position within the box. You can use the arrow keys, or drag with the mouse, to move the image.
Rotate	Rotates the image within the box. When you select this command, a rotation axis is displayed on the figure. Point at the right end of the axis and drag to the new angle. If you click anywhere on the figure, the axis rotates so the right end of the axis points at that location. To rotate without selecting the Rotate command, press Ctrl+← or Ctrl+→.
Scale	Changes the size of the image in the box (not the box size). Select Enlarge % or Reduce % to enlarge or reduce the size by a fixed percent (shown on the status bar). Select Enlarge Area to zoom in on an area of the figure with the mouse. Select Reset Size to return the image to its original size.

Mirror	Flips the image about its vertical axis to create a mirror image.
Invert	Converts each color in the image to its complementary color (for example, blue to orange). Black and white are not affected.
Outline	Displays the image as a line drawing. All colors in the image become white (black remains black).
Black and White	Changes all colors in the image to black; white remains white.
Edit All	Displays a dialog box in which you can enter exact values for various editing options.
Reset All	Returns the image to its original state (that is, undoes all your changes).

TO WORK WITH IMAGE FILES

The following commands are found on the Figure Editor File menu.

Retrieve	Reads a graphics image from disk into the Figure Editor. The retrieved image will replace the existing image in the editor and in the document figure box.
Save As	Saves the image being edited as a WPG (WordPerfect Graphic) format file on disk. Does not save editing changes with the image.
Graphic On Disk	Saves the image with editing changes on disk.
Box Position	Changes the position and size of the graphics box in the document. See the Graphics Boxes entry for more information.
Cancel	Closes the Figure Editor without saving your changes.
Close	Closes the Figure Editor and saves your changes.

F

NOTES To hide, display, or modify the Figure Editor Button Bar, select commands from the View menu.

When you edit an image, the editing changes are saved with the document and not made part of the original graphics image file on disk. To save a version of the image that includes the editing changes, use the File ➤ Graphic On Disk command.

See Also Graphics Boxes

FILE MANAGER

The File Manager provides a variety of file manipulation features. You can move, copy, and delete files; search document files for word patterns; create subdirectories; and so on. Strictly speaking, the File Manager is not part of WordPerfect for Windows but is a separate program. It is very powerful, and even cursory coverage of all its features is beyond the scope of this book. This section covers only a few of the most important File Manager tasks.

The File Manager has its own menus and Button Bar. When you first start the File Manager, the top portion of the screen, called the *Navigator*, displays several small windows, or *panes*, that list your system's drives and directories. You use the Navigator to make selections of directories and files. The lower portion of the screen is the *Viewer*, which displays the contents of the selected file.

TO USE THE FILE MANAGER

1. From the main WordPerfect for Windows menu select File ➤ File Manager.
2. Use the File Manager menus and Button Bar to select the desired operations.
3. When finished, select File ➤ Exit or press Alt+F4 to close the File Manager.

TO VIEW AND OPEN A DOCUMENT FILE

1. Use the Navigator to access the desired directory. The directory's files will be listed in one of the panes.
2. Select the desired file. Its contents will be displayed in the Viewer. Select additional files to view, if necessary.

3. If you want to open the current file for editing (assuming it's a Word-Perfect for Windows document), select File ➤ Open or click the Open button.

TO MOVE/RENAME OR COPY A FILE

1. Select the desired file in the Navigator.
2. To copy the file to a different disk/directory, select File ➤ Copy, press Ctrl+C, or click the Copy button. To move or rename the file, select File ➤ Move/Rename, press Ctrl+R, or click the Move button.
3. In the dialog box, enter the file destination or its new name, and then press ↵.

TO SEARCH FOR TEXT IN FILES

1. In the Navigator, display the directory containing the files to be searched.
2. Select Search ➤ Find Words or click the Find Word button.
3. In the dialog box enter the words or other text to search for, and then select Find or press ↵.
4. The File Manager searches the selected files and displays a list of all files that contain the search text. If you select a file in this list, its contents will be displayed in the Viewer.

NOTES Please see your program documentation for additional information on the many capabilities of the File Manager.

FONT

PURPOSE To control the font (typeface and size) and appearance of text in a document.

TO SELECT A FONT

1. Select the text to change, or move the insertion point to the location for the new font to begin.

2. Select Font ➤ Font or press F9. The Font dialog box is displayed.

3. In the Font and Point Size list boxes, select the name and size of the new font. The lower box shows a sample of text in the selected font and size.

4. In the Appearance section select one or more appearance options, if desired.

5. Select OK or press ↵.

TO CHANGE FONT SIZE

1. Select the text to change.

2. Select Font ➤ Size or press Ctrl+S. The Size menu is displayed.

3. Select the desired size.

NOTES The specific fonts available depend on your printer.

If the Ruler is displayed, you can click the Font button to specify fonts (but only those fonts that have been assigned to the Ruler).

See Also Default Initial Codes, Document Initial Codes, Ruler

FOOTERS

See Headers and Footers

FOOTNOTES

PURPOSE To print a footnote at the bottom of the page where it is referred to in the text. Footnotes are not displayed during editing but are printed and can be viewed on the Print Preview screen.

TO CREATE A FOOTNOTE

1. Move the insertion point to the location in the document where you want the footnote number.

2. Select Layout ➤ Footnote ➤ Create. The Footnote window opens wih the footnote number already inserted.

3. Enter the text of the footnote. You can use most of the WordPerfect for Windows editing and formatting commands in a footnote.

4. Select Close. The footnote number is inserted in the text. The footnote text will be printed at the bottom of the page.

TO EDIT A FOOTNOTE

1. Select Layout ➤ Footnote ➤ Edit. The Edit Footnote dialog box is displayed.

2. Enter the number of the note you want to edit and press ↵. The Footnote screen opens with the selected footnote displayed for editing.

3. Make the desired changes, and then select Close.

TO MODIFY FOOTNOTE OPTIONS

1. Select Layout ➤ Footnote ➤ Options. The Footnote Options dialog box is displayed.

2. Open the Numbering Method pop-up list and select the numbering method. Select Numbers (the default) for sequential numbers. Select Letters for sequential letters (a, b, c, and so on). Select Characters to use the character you enter in the Characters text box. The character will be used by itself for the first footnote, then doubled, and so on (*, **, ***, etc.). Select the Restart Numbering option to have footnote numbering start at 1 on each page.

3. The Style in Text box specifies how the footnote number appears in the body of the document. The Style in Note box specifies how the number appears in the footnote. In both, the [Note Num] code represents the number itself. To enter codes in these boxes, open the pop-up list for each one.

4. The Line Spacing in Notes setting controls the spacing of lines within notes. The Spacing Between Notes settings controls the amount of blank space inserted between consecutive notes on the same page.

5. Open the Position pop-up list to specify where footnotes are printed on pages when the text does not fill the page. The After Text option positions the footnotes immediately after the end of the text, and the Bottom of Page option (the default) positions them at the bottom of the page.

6. Open the Separator pop-up list to select the type of separator that will be placed between the text and the footnotes. You can choose a two-inch line (the default), a margin-to-margin line, or no line.

7. When all options are set as you want them, select OK or press ↵.

TO CHANGE FOOTNOTE NUMBERING

1. Move the insertion point to where you want the new footnote numbering to start.

2. Select Layout ➤ Footnotes ➤ New Number. The New Number dialog box is displayed.

3. Enter the new footnote number, and then select OK or press ↵.

NOTES To delete a footnote, use the Reveal Codes window to find the Footnote code, and delete it.

See Also Default Initial Codes, Endnotes, Headers and Footers

FORMATTING CODES

PURPOSE To control document formatting. When you issue formatting commands, WordPerfect for Windows inserts the corresponding formatting codes in the document. Normally you do not see these codes, only their effects on the document's appearance. By deleting a formatting code, you remove its effect.

TO VIEW FORMATTING CODES

1. Press Alt+F3 or select View ➤ Reveal Codes.

2. The Reveal Codes window opens on the lower portion of the screen. Both text and codes are shown in this window.

3. To close the Reveal Codes window, press Alt+F3 or select View ➤ Reveal Codes.

TO DELETE FORMATTING CODES

1. Press Alt+F3 or select View ➤ Reveal Codes to open the Reveal Codes window.
2. Use the mouse or the arrow keys to move the highlight to the desired code.
3. Press Del.

NOTES Some formatting codes always work in pairs. An "on" code turns the formatting option on, and an "off" code turns it off. Only text between the two codes is affected. If you delete one of a pair of codes, the other is deleted automatically. Examples of paired codes are Boldface, Italics, and Underline.

Other codes work alone. They affect text from their location to the end of the document, or up to another code that modifies that formatting. Example of single codes are Margins, Font, and Justification.

GO TO

PURPOSE To move the insertion point to a specific location in the document.

TO GO TO A SPECIFIC LOCATION

1. Select Edit ➤ Go To or press Ctrl+G.

2. In the Go To dialog box select the desired option:

- To go to a specific page, enter the page number, and then press ↵.

- To go to the top or bottom of the current page, open the Position pop-up list, select the destination, and then press ↵.

- To go to the previous insertion point position, select Last Position.

See Also Insertion Point

GRAPHICS BOXES

PURPOSE To create *graphics boxes* in your document. A graphics box can contain a diagram, an equation, a table, or text. The contents of a graphics box are independent from the regular text in a document, and can be moved, sized, and edited as needed. If a graphics box is less than full page wide, document text will automatically be formatted to flow around the box.

There are five types of graphics boxes: figure box, table box, equation box, text box, and user box. WordPerfect for Windows automatically maintains a numbered list for each box type. For example, if the first graphics box in a document is a figure box, it will be *Figure 1*; if the second graphics box is a table box, it will be *Table 1*. You can also use the List feature to create separate lists of each box type. The type of a box does not restrict its contents; you can place figures, tables, equations, or text in any kind of box. Generally, however, each box type is used for certain kinds of elements:

- Figure boxes are used for graphic images, charts, and diagrams. WordPerfect for Windows can import images in a variety of file formats, letting you use figures created with different applications.

- Equation boxes are used for mathematical and scientific equations. You can create and edit equations using the Equation Editor.

◆ Text boxes are used for sidebars, quotes, and other text you want set off from the main document body. You can retrieve a file into a text box or enter text from the keyboard.

◆ Table boxes are used to hold WordPerfect tables. A table need not be placed in a box, but doing so gives you additional flexibility in positioning the table.

◆ User boxes are a general catchall category, used for elements that don't fit any of the above categories.

When you create a box, it is inserted in the document at the location of the insertion point. Figure, table, and text boxes are visible in the document even when empty; user and equation boxes are not visible unless they contain something.

TO CREATE A FIGURE BOX

1. Select Graphics ➤ Figure ➤ Create. The Figure Editor screen is displayed with an empty box.

2. To add an empty box to the document (into which you can later insert a figure), go to step 3. To insert a figure now, select File ➤ Retrieve, enter or select the name of the graphics file, and then select Retrieve.

3. Select File ➤ Close to insert the box and return to the document.

TO CREATE A TEXT BOX

1. Select Graphics ➤ Text Box ➤ Create or press Alt+F11. The Text Box Editor screen is displayed.

2. To add an empty box to the document (into which you can later insert text), go to step 3. To insert text now, enter text and formatting in the usual manner. To read a file into the text box, select File ➤ Retrieve, specify the file name, and then select Retrieve.

3. Select File ➤ Close to insert the box and return to the document.

TO CREATE AN EQUATION BOX

1. Select Graphics ➤ Equation ➤ Create. The Equation Editor screen is displayed.

2. Create an equation, or read one from disk by selecting File ➤ Retrieve, typing or selecting the equation name, and then selecting Retrieve.

3. Select File ➤ Close to insert the box and return to the document.

TO CREATE A TABLE OR USER BOX

1. Select either Graphics ➤ Table Box or Graphics ➤ User Box, and then select Create.

2. In the dialog box select which editor (Figure Editor, Text Box Editor, or Equation Editor) you want to use, and then select OK to open the editor.

3. Create the box contents or retrieve them from disk using the procedures explained above. You can use the table commands to create a table.

4. Select File ➤ Close to insert the box and return to the document.

TO EDIT THE CONTENTS OF A GRAPHICS BOX

1. Select Graphics, and then select the type of box to edit. Select Edit and enter the number of the box to edit. With the mouse, double-click the box you want to edit.

2. Depending on the box contents, either the Figure Editor, Equation Editor, or Text Box Editor will be opened. See the corresponding entries for information on using the editors.

3. Make the desired changes, and then exit the editor.

TO DELETE A BOX

◆ Select the box by clicking it, and then press Del.

or

◆ Delete the box code on the Reveal Codes screen.

TO CREATE OR EDIT A BOX CAPTION

If a box has a caption, the caption will display below the box and wrap to match the box width by default.

1. Select Graphics, select the box type, and then select Caption. Enter the number of the box whose caption you want to create or edit. You can also

click on the box with the right mouse button, and then select Edit Caption. To edit an existing caption, you can double-click the caption.

2. The Caption Editor screen opens. If the box already has a caption, the caption is displayed. If not, the box number is displayed in the upper-left corner of the editor screen. You can use this number, or delete it if you don't want the caption to include a number. To reinsert the box number, select Box Number.

3. Enter the caption text, or select File ➤ Retrieve to read a disk file into the caption. You can use most of the WordPerfect for Windows editing and formatting commands in the Caption Editor.

4. Select Close to save the caption, or Cancel to exit without saving changes.

TO MODIFY THE
APPEARANCE OF GRAPHICS BOXES

When you modify the appearance of a graphics box, the changes apply to all graphics boxes of the specified type from the position of the insertion point onward.

1. Position the insertion point where you want the changes to take effect.

2. Select Graphics, select the type of box whose appearance you want to change, and then select Options.

3. Make the desired changes in the dialog box. The most important settings are as follows:

- The Border Styles section lets you specify the type of line that will be used for each of the four edges of the box.

- The Border Spacing section specifies the amount of space between each border of the box and elements inside and outside the box.

- Gray Shading specifies the background shading for the box: 0% is no shading, 100% is black.

- In the Caption Numbering section you can specify the format and style of the box numbers.

- The Caption Position pop-up list lets you select the caption position relative to the box.

4. Once all appearance options have been set, select OK or press ↵.

TO MODIFY THE POSITION AND SIZE OF GRAPHICS BOXES

You can change a graphics box's size and position with a dialog box or with the mouse. These techniques are discussed in turn.

WITH A DIALOG BOX

1. Select Graphics and select the type of box whose position and size you want to change. Select Position, and then enter the number of the box to modify. With the mouse, click on the box with the right button, and then select Position. The Position and Size dialog box is displayed.

2. Make the desired changes in the dialog box, as follows:

- The Box Type pop-up list lets you change the type of the box.

- The Vertical Position and Horizontal Position options specify the position of the box with respect to its anchor (see below).

- Anchor To controls the document element that the box is anchored to, and how the box moves when text is moved. The options are as follows:

Page	The box's position is fixed on the page.
Paragraph	The box moves with the paragraph it's in.
Character	The box moves with the line it's in.

- The Size section lets you control box size precisely. You have four options:

Auto Height	You enter the box width and the proportional height is calculated.
Auto Width	You enter the box height and the proportional width is calculated.
Auto Both	Both height and width are calculated to match the image's original dimensions.
Set Both	You enter both width and height.

- The Wrap Text Around Box option determines whether document text wraps around the box or prints over the box.

3. When all position options are set as desired, select OK or press ↵.

WITH THE MOUSE

1. To move a graphics box, point at it (the mouse pointer will change to a four-headed arrow). Then simply drag the box to the new position.

2. To resize a graphics box, click it. Small black rectangles called *sizing handles* will be displayed around the box. Point at one of the handles (the mouse pointer will change to a two-headed arrow) and drag the outline to the desired size.

NOTES WordPerfect for Windows can retrieve graphics files in the following formats:

EXTENSION	TYPE
BMP	Windows 3.*x* bitmap
CGM	Computer Graphics Metafile
DHP	Dr. Halo PIC
DXF	AutoCAD
EPS	Encapsulated PostScript
GEM	GEM Draw
HPGL	Hewlett Packard Graphics Language Plotter File
IMG	GEM Paint
MSP	Windows (2.*x*) Paint
PCX	PC Paintbrush
PIC	Lotus 1-2-3 PIC
PNTG	Macintosh Paint
PPIC	PC Paint Plus
TIFF	Tagged Image File
WMF	Windows Metafile
WPG	WordPerfect Graphics

WordPerfect for Windows includes a library of several dozen images (in WPG format) that you can use in your documents.

If the Wrap Text Around Box option is off for a box, you cannot select the box by clicking it with the left mouse button. Instead, you must click the box with the right mouse button, and then choose Select Box from the menu that is displayed.

See Also Default Initial Codes, Equation Editor, Figure Editor, Tables, Text Box Editor

H

HARD PAGE BREAK

PURPOSE To force a new page to begin at a specific location.

TO INSERT A HARD PAGE BREAK

1. Move the insertion point to the location for the new page to begin.

2. Press Ctrl+↵.

NOTES A hard page break is indicated on the screen by a double horizontal line.

HEADERS AND FOOTERS

PURPOSE To display and print text at the top or bottom of every page.

TO CREATE A HEADER

1. Move the insertion point to the first page you want the header displayed on.

2. Select Layout ➤ Page or press Alt+F9.

3. Select Headers. The Headers dialog box is displayed.

4. Select Header A for the first header you create. Select Header B if you're creating a second header for alternate pages.

5. Select Create. The header editing screen is opened. This screen is very similar to the normal editing screen, and almost all editing commands function in the same way.

6. Type in the header text, and format the header as desired. To insert the page number in the header, select the Page Number button. A page number code (^B) is inserted in the header at the insertion point.

7. The header is displayed and printed on every page by default. To have the header displayed/printed only on odd or even numbered pages, select the Placement button, and then specify the desired placement.

8. Once the header is complete, select Close.

TO CREATE A FOOTER

Follow the procedures for creating a header, except in step 3 select Footers.

TO EDIT A HEADER

1. If your document includes two or more headers, move the insertion point just past the header code. If necessary use the Search feature to find the code.
2. Select Layout ➤ Page or press Alt+F9.
3. Select Headers, and then select A or B.
4. Select Edit. The header editing screen opens with the existing header displayed.
5. Make the desired changes in the header, and then select Close.

TO EDIT A FOOTER

Follow the procedures for editing a header, except in step 3 select Footers.

TO DISCONTINUE A HEADER OR FOOTER

1. Move the insertion point to the first page where the header or footer is to be discontinued.
2. Select Layout ➤ Page or press Alt+F9.
3. Select Headers or Footers.
4. Select A or B, and then select Discontinue.

NOTES If your document contains only a single header or footer, the insertion point can be at any location when you edit the header or footer.

Once a header or footer has been discontinued you cannot simply "re-continue" it, but rather must create a new header or footer.

See Also Endnotes, Footnotes

HELP

PURPOSE To provide a help system that you can use to obtain on-screen information about program commands and operations. Help information is displayed in a window that, like any other window, can be moved, sized, and so on.

TO OBTAIN HELP ABOUT A MENU COMMAND OR DIALOG BOX

1. To get help about any dialog box, display the dialog box. To get help about a menu command, display the menu and highlight the command.
2. Press F1.

TO ACCESS THE HELP INDEX

1. Select Help ➤ Index, or press F1 while the editing screen is displayed.
2. Click a letter to move to that section of the index, or scroll in the window to view an alphabetical list of all Help topics.
3. Click on a topic to view relevant information.

TO ACCESS THE FULL HELP SYSTEM

1. Select Help from the menu bar.
2. From the Help menu make one of the following selections:

   ◆ Select Index to access the Help index.

   ◆ Select Keyboard for information on keyboard layouts and keystrokes.

   ◆ Select How Do I for information on how to perform commonly needed tasks.

   ◆ Select Glossary for an alphabetical listing of definitions.

   ◆ Select Using Help for information on how to use the Help system.

   ◆ Select What Is for context-sensitive help on screen regions and keystrokes. The mouse pointer changes into an arrow with a question mark. Click on any screen region, or press any non-typing key or key combination, to view related information.

- Select About WordPerfect to view information about the program version number and release date.

TO NAVIGATE THE HELP WINDOWS

When the Help system is active, there are several methods you can use for moving around Help to find the information you need. Some of these methods use the buttons displayed at the top of the Help window, and others involve special terms that are underlined in the help text.

- To go to the Help index, select Index.
- To go back to the last help topic viewed, select Back.
- To move forward or backward through predefined sequences of related help topics, select Browse → or Browse ←. If you are at the end or beginning of a sequence, one of the Browse buttons will be grayed.
- To search for a particular help topic, select Search.
- A word with a solid underline in the help text is a *jump term*. You can move directly to the jump term topic by clicking the word. You can also highlight the word by pressing Tab or Shift+Tab, and then pressing ↵.
- A word with a dotted underline is a glossary entry. Point at the word and press and hold the mouse button to view a pop-up definition of the word. Or, highlight the word by pressing Tab or Shift+Tab, and then press and hold ↵.

TO USE THE HELP MENUS

The Help window has several menu commands that provide additional features:

- Select File ➤ Print Topic to print the current Help topic.
- Select Edit ➤ Copy to copy the current Help topic to the clipboard (you do not need to highlight text first—the entire topic is automatically copied). You can then return to the document and paste the information into a document window for viewing and modification.
- Select Edit ➤ Annotate to add your own annotation to a Help topic. An annotated topic is displayed with a paper clip symbol next to the topic name. Select the paper clip (as you would select a jump term) to view the annotation.

- Select Bookmark ➤ Define to place a bookmark on a Help topic that you refer to frequently. To move directly to a bookmarked topic, select Bookmark, and then select the desired topic.

- Select Help to obtain information about using the Help system.

HYPHENATION

PURPOSE To hyphenate automatically words that would otherwise extend past the right margin.

TO TURN HYPHENATION ON

1. Move the insertion point to the document location where you want hyphenation to start.

2. Select Layout ➤ Line or press Shift+F9, and then select Hyphenation. The Line Hyphenation dialog box is displayed.

3. Select the Hyphenation On option, and then select OK or press ↵.

TO CONTROL THE HYPHENATION ZONE

The hyphenation zone controls when words are hyphenated. The zone straddles the right margin, extending a certain distance to the left and to the right of the margin. Only words that span the entire hyphenation zone will be hyphenated. A wider hyphenation zone results in fewer words being hyphenated.

1. Select Layout ➤ Line or press Shift+F9, and then select Hyphenation. The Line Hyphenation dialog box is displayed.

2. Enter the desired values for the left and right sections of the hyphenation zone. The values are expressed as a percentage of the line length. With a 6.5 inch line, the default settings of 10% left and 4% right give a hyphenation zone that extends 0.65 inch to the left of the margin and 0.26 inch to the right of the margin.

3. Select OK or press ↵.

TO WORK WITH HYPHENATION

When a word needs to be hyphenated, WordPerfect for Windows looks through its hyphenation dictionary. If the word is found, the hyphen is inserted accordingly. If WordPerfect for Windows needs help in placing the hyphen, the Position Hyphen dialog box is displayed. In this dialog box you have several choices (see the Notes section for information on the types of hyphen codes):

- To make the word wrap to the next line instead of being hyphenated, select Ignore Word.

- To insert a hyphen at a certain position in the word, click at that position (or use the ← and → keys), and then select Insert Hyphen.

- To insert a hyphenation soft return at a certain position in the word, click at that position (or use the ← and → keys), and then select Hyphenation SRT.

- To insert a space at a certain position in the word, click at that position (or use the ← and → keys), and then select Insert Space.

TO CONTROL HYPHENATION OPTIONS

You can control the way WordPerfect for Windows acts when it encounters a word that needs hyphenation. Select File ➤ Preferences ➤ Environment. In the dialog box select the desired option under Prompt for Hyphenation:

- Select Never to have the word hyphenated according to the dictionary if the word is found, or wrapped to the next line if not found.

- Select When Required (the default) to have the word hyphenated according to the dictionary if the word is found, or to prompt you for help if not found.

- Select Always to have the program prompt you for every word that needs hyphenation.

NOTES WordPerfect for Windows uses several types of hyphenation codes. You insert these special codes in your document by selecting Layout ➤ Line ➤ Special Codes, and then selecting the desired code from the dialog box. Some codes can be inserted with shortcut keys, as explained below.

- A *regular hyphen* is a code ([–]) that you insert by pressing the – key (minus sign). Even though it's a code, it displays on the editing screen. This kind of hyphen breaks a word at the right margin when necessary, and also displays when the word does not necessarily need to be broken,

but is always spelled with a hyphen. Use a regular hyphen in words such as *well-known*.

◆ A *soft hyphen* is a code (–) that you insert by pressing Ctrl+Shift+–. A soft hyphen breaks a word at the right margin when necessary. It displays only when the word is broken.

◆ A *dash* is a character, not a code. You insert it by pressing Ctrl+–. It behaves like any other character, and it does not break words at the right margin.

◆ A *hyphenation soft return* is like a soft hyphen in that it breaks a word at the right margin. It does not, however, display as a hyphen. The hyphenation soft return is often used in words separated by slashes.

See Also Default Initial Codes

IMPORTING FILES

PURPOSE To open a file in a non-WordPerfect format.

TO IMPORT A FILE

1. Select File ➤ Open, press F4, or click the Open button on the Button Bar.
2. If you know the filename, you can type it into the Filename text box.
3. Select the desired file from the Files list box. Use the Directories list box to change to another drive and/or directory, if needed.
4. Press ↵ or select Open. If the file is not in WordPerfect 5.0 or 5.1 format, the Convert File Format dialog box is displayed.
5. WordPerfect for Windows chooses a convert format based on information in the file. Select a different convert format if you know that WordPerfect's choice is incorrect.
6. Select OK or press ↵.

NOTES Depending on the original file format, WordPerfect for Windows may not be able to convert all document formatting correctly.

See Also Exporting Files, Figure Editor, Graphics Boxes, Opening a File

INDENTATION

PURPOSE To control the spacing between a paragraph's lines of text and the left and right margins.

TO CHANGE INDENTATION

Indentation is usually applied to an entire paragraph. To indent an existing paragraph, move the insertion point to the left end of the first line, and then enter the desired indent command. To indent a new paragraph, press ↵, enter the desired indent command, and then start typing the paragraph. The four indent commands are as follows:

Tab Indent	Press Tab. The first line is indented from the left margin.
Indent	Press F7. All lines are indented from the left margin.
Double indent	Press Ctrl+Shift+F7. All lines are indented from the left and right margins.
Hanging indent	Press Ctrl+F7. All lines except the first are indented from the left margin.

NOTES All of the indent commands (except Tab indent) can also be entered via the menus, by selecting Layout ➤ Paragraph, and then selecting the desired indent. Indentation aligns with tab stops.

See Also Tabs

INDEX

PURPOSE To create an alphabetical list of a document's topics with references to the relevant page numbers. Creating an index for a document is a three-step process. First you specify words or phrases to be included in the index, by marking them in the document or by creating a concordance file that contains them. Next you define the document location and format of the index. Finally you generate the index.

TO SPECIFY INDEX ENTRIES MANUALLY

1. Select the word or phrase you want in the index.
2. Select Tools ➤ Mark Text or press F12, and then select Index. The Mark Index dialog box is displayed with the selected text in the Heading box.
3. If you want to mark the selected text as a heading in the index, select OK or press ↵.

4. If you want the selected text marked as a subheading, type the desired heading into the Heading box, and then select the Subheading text box. The selected text (from the document) will be entered in the Subheading box. Select OK or press ↵.

TO CREATE A CONCORDANCE FILE

1. Start with a blank document.

2. Type in each index entry on its own line. An entry can be more than one line long, but each one must end with a hard return.

3. Each entry in the concordance is used as a heading in the index. To specify a subheading, mark the concordance entry as a subheading using the technique explained above.

4. Save the file, and then specify it as the concordance file when defining the index (see below).

TO DEFINE THE INDEX

1. Move the insertion point to the location where you want the index located. This will usually be at the end of the document after a hard page break.

2. Select Tools ➤ Define or press Shift+F12, and then select Index. The Define Index dialog box is displayed.

3. Open the Numbering Format pop-up list and select the desired format for the index. The box below shows a sample of the currently selected format.

4. If you are using a concordance file instead of or in addition to manually marked text, enter the filename in the Optional Concordance File box.

5. Select OK.

TO GENERATE THE INDEX

1. Select Tools ➤ Generate or press Alt+F12, and then select Yes.

2. WordPerfect will generate the index and all other addenda in the document (table of contents and lists). A dialog box keeps you informed of progress.

NOTES For entries that occur frequently in your document, it is easier to create a concordance file than to mark text manually. You can use a concordance file and manual text marking together for the same index.

When using a concordance file, every document occurrence of each concordance entry is included in the index. The matching process is exact ("profit" will not match "profits"), but it is not case sensitive.

When marking text manually, you must mark every instance of a word or phrase that you want in the index.

Index generation will be faster if the entries in your concordance file are sorted into alphabetical order (see the Sort entry).

See Also Lists, Sort, Table of Contents

INITIAL CODES

See Default Initial Codes and Document Initial Codes

INITIAL FONT

PURPOSE To control the document's default font.

TO SPECIFY THE INITIAL FONT

1. Select Layout ➤ Document or press Ctrl+Shift+F9.
2. Select Initial Font.
3. In the Font and Point Size list boxes, the name and size of the current initial font are highlighted. The lower box shows a sample of text in the highlighted font and size.
4. Select a different font name and/or size; the sample box shows you what it looks like.
5. Once the desired font and size are highlighted, select OK.

See Also Document Initial Codes, Font

INSERTION POINT

PURPOSE To mark where editing actions occur.

TO MOVE THE INSERTION POINT

Use the following keys and key combinations to move the insertion point around in your document:

←	Left one character
→	Right one character
↑	Up one line
↓	Down one line
Ctrl+←	Left one word
Ctrl+→	Right one word
Home	Beginning of line (after codes)
Home,Home	Beginning of line (before codes)
End	End of line (after codes)
PgUp	Top of screen, and then up a screen at a time
PgDn	Bottom of screen, and then down a screen at a time
Alt+PgUp	First line on previous page
Alt+PgDn	First line on next page
Ctrl+↓	Down one paragraph
Ctrl+↑	Up one paragraph
Ctrl+Home	Beginning of document (after codes)
Ctrl+Home, Ctrl+Home	Beginning of document (before codes)
Ctrl+End	End of document

NOTES With the mouse, you can move the insertion point by clicking the new location. If necessary, first use the scroll bar to bring the desired location on the screen.

ITALICS

TO ITALICIZE EXISTING TEXT

1. Select the text.

2. Select Font ➤ Italic or press Ctrl+I.

TO ITALICIZE AS YOU TYPE

1. Select Font ➤ Italic or press Ctrl+I to begin italics.

2. Type in the text.

3. Select Font ➤ Italic or press Ctrl+I again to end italics.

NOTES Italics can be combined with bold, underlining, and other font attributes.

See Also Selecting Text

JUSTIFICATION

PURPOSE To control the way text is lined up at the left and right margins of the page.

TO CHANGE JUSTIFICATION

1. Move the insertion point to the place where you want the new justification to start.

2. Select Layout ➤ Justification, and then select Left, Right, Center, or Full. You can also use the shortcut keys: Ctrl+L (left), Ctrl+R (right), Ctrl+J (center), and Ctrl+F (full).

NOTES The four justification options are as follows:

Left	Text is aligned at the left margin, but it is not aligned (that is, it's *ragged*) at the right margin. This is the default.
Right	Text is aligned at the right margin and ragged at the left margin.
Full	Text is aligned both left and right.
Center	Text is centered on the line, and it is ragged at the left and right margins.

NOTES If the Ruler is displayed, you can click the Justification button to select from the four justification options.

See Also Default Initial Codes, Margins, Ruler

KEYBOARD LAYOUTS

PURPOSE To select the keyboard layout.

TO SELECT A KEYBOARD LAYOUT

1. Select File ➤ Preferences ➤ Keyboard. The Keyboard dialog box is displayed with the name of the keyboard layout currently in use.

2. To change layouts, choose the Select button. Then from the list, select the desired keyboard and press ↵.

3. To return to the default Common User Access layout, select Default (CUA).

4. Select OK.

NOTES The default Common User Access keyboard layout provides key assignments that are similar to those in other Windows applications. The other predefined keyboard layouts are as follows (see your program documentation for further details):

- wpdos51.wwk provides a keyboard layout like that used in the DOS version of WordPerfect 5.1.

- equation.wwk provides a layout designed for working with the equation editor.

- equdos51.wwk provides an equation layout like that used in the DOS version of WordPerfect 5.1.

- macros.wwk provides a layout for use with macros.

LANGUAGE

PURPOSE To tailor certain program features to a specific language.

TO SPECIFY THE LANGUAGE IN USE

1. Move the insertion point to the location where the new language starts.

2. Select Tools ➤ Language, and then select the desired language from the list.

3. Select OK or press ↵.

NOTES To specify a different language for all aspects of a document, including footnotes, you must insert the New Language code in the document's initial codes.

When you specify a different language, the language chosen affects certain aspects of program function, such as sort order and date format. It also affects spell checking and thesaurus operations, but only if you have the dictionary and thesaurus files for the specified language.

See Also Date, Default Initial Codes, Document Initial Codes, Sort, Speller, Thesaurus

LAYOUT

See Headers and Footers, Page Numbering, Paper Size

LINE DRAW

PURPOSE To draw vertical lines, horizontal lines, and boxes using any character.

TO DRAW LINES

1. Move the insertion point to where you want the line to begin.

2. Select Tools ➤ Line Draw or press Ctrl+D. The screen switches to Draft display mode, and the Line Draw dialog box is displayed.

3. Use the mouse to select one of the ten preset characters.

4. Use the arrow keys to draw lines. As you draw, the dialog box remains displayed.

5. To move the insertion point without drawing, select Move. To erase lines, select Erase. To return to drawing mode, select Draw.

6. Select Close when finished.

NOTES Lines you draw will overwrite existing text. An arrow at the end of a line means that the line does not connect to another line, and that the line segment is 1 half-space long. To convert a half-space line into a full-space line, press Alt+End.

The following quick-draw keystrokes can be used to extend a line from the insertion point to a margin quickly:

- ◆ Home or Ctrl+←To the left margin
- ◆ End or Ctrl+→To the right margin
- ◆ Ctrl+↑To the top margin
- ◆ Ctrl+↓To the bottom margin

When you draw an empty box with Line Draw, the "empty" space within the box is actually filled with spaces and hard returns. To keep such a box intact while you place text in it (in regular editing mode) you must press Ins to activate Insert mode.

LINE SPACING

PURPOSE To control the vertical spacing between lines.

TO CHANGE LINE SPACING

1. Move the insertion point to where you want the new spacing to begin.

2. Select Layout ➤ Line or press Shift+F9.

3. Select Spacing.

4. Enter the desired spacing in the text box, or use the ↑ and ↓ keys to increase or decrease the spacing by 0. 5 at a time. You can also use the

mouse to click the up and down arrows next to the text box to increase or decrease the spacing.

5. Select OK or press ⏎.

NOTE If the Ruler is displayed, you can click the Line Spacing button to select a spacing of 1, 1.5, or 2.

See Also Ruler

LINK

PURPOSE To link data into a WordPerfect for Windows document from any other Windows application that supports Dynamic Data Exchange (DDE). When the original data changes, the linked copy in the WordPerfect document is automatically updated.

TO PASTE A LINK INTO A DOCUMENT

1. The source application and WordPerfect for Windows must both be open.

2. Switch to the application containing the source file, and copy the data to the clipboard.

3. Switch to the WordPerfect for Windows document and move the insertion point to the location where you want the linked data inserted.

4. Select Edit ➤ Link ➤ Paste Link. The data is pasted into the document, and a link to the source file is established. Comments are inserted in the document to mark the start and end of the linked data.

TO CREATE A LINK TO AN OPEN SOURCE FILE MANUALLY

1. Move the insertion point to the location where you want the linked data inserted.

2. Select Edit ➤ Link ➤ Create. A dialog box is displayed listing all source applications and filenames from which you can link data.

3. Select the desired application/file; its name will be transferred to the text line at the top of the list box.

4. To link the entire source file, proceed to step 5. To link only a portion of the data in the source file, enter a vertical bar (|) at the end of the filename followed by the name of the data item or section (for example, a named range in a spreadsheet).

5. Type a name for the link in the Link Name text box.

6. Under Update Mode select Manual or Automatic (see the Notes section).

7. Under Storage Type select Text or Graphics (see the Notes section).

8. Select OK or press ↵.

TO CREATE A LINK TO A SOURCE FILE THAT IS NOT OPEN

1. Move the insertion point to the location where you want the linked data inserted.

2. Select Edit ➤ Link ➤ Create. A dialog box is displayed listing all open source applications and filenames. Since your source application is not open, it will not be on this list.

3. Type the desired application and filename (separated by a vertical line) in the text line at the top of the list box.

4. To link the entire source file, proceed to step 5. To link only a portion of the data in the source file, enter a vertical bar (|) at the end of the filename followed by the name of the data item or section (for example, a named range in a spreadsheet).

5. Type a name for the link in the Link Name text box.

6. Under Update Mode select Manual or Automatic (see the Notes section).

7. Under Storage Type select Text or Graphics (see the Notes section).

8. Select OK or press ↵. Link codes are inserted in the document but the data is not transferred until both files are open.

NOTES When you select Automatic Update, the link is updated automatically whenever both source and destination files are open and the source data has changed. If you select Manual Update you must select Edit ➤ Link ➤ Update (with both files open) to update a link.

Select Text as the storage type to have the linked data inserted as text in your document. Select Graphics as the storage type to have the linked data stored in a graphics box. Some source data can be stored only as text or as graphics regardless of the storage type you select.

Refer to the documentation for your other DDE applications for information on naming data items and sections.

LISTS

PURPOSE To create lists with page number references in a document automatically. The procedure involves three steps. You first mark the document text to be included in the list. Next, you define the location and numbering format of the list. Finally you generate the list.

TO MARK TEXT TO INCLUDE IN THE LIST

1. Select the text to be included in the list.

2. Select Tools ➤ Mark Text or press F12, and then select List. The Mark List dialog box is displayed.

3. If you are creating only a single list, select OK or press ↵. If you are creating multiple lists, open the Number pop-up box and select the list:

- Select List 1–5 to include the text in a regular list.

- Select List 6–10 to include the text in a list that will also automatically include graphics captions (see the Notes section).

4. Select OK or press ↵.

TO DEFINE A LIST

1. Position the insertion point at the location in the document where you want the list.

2. Select Tools ➤ Define or press Shift+F12, and then select List. The Define List dialog box is displayed.

3. Open the List pop-up box and select the list (1–10) you are defining. If a list has already been defined in the document, it will have a checkmark next to it in the pop-up box.

4. Use the Numbering Format pop-up box to select the numbering format for the list. The lower box shows you a sample of the selected format.

5. Select OK or press ↵.

TO GENERATE LISTS

1. Select Tools ➤ Generate or press Alt+F12, and then select Yes.

2. WordPerfect will generate all lists and other addenda (index and table of contents) in the document. A dialog box keeps you informed of progress.

NOTES Lists are typically used to refer readers to the locations of tables and illustrations in a document.

You can have as many as ten independent lists in a document. Lists 1–5 are general purpose lists and will contain only the text you specifically mark in the document. Lists 6–10 are predefined to contain the captions of graphical document elements: list 6, Figure captions; list 7, Table captions; list 8, Text box captions; list 9, User Box captions; list 10, Equation captions. Lists 6–10 can also contain any text you specifically mark for inclusion. For example, list 6 will contain the captions of all figures as well as any document text that you specifically mark for list 6.

See Also Index, Table of Contents

MACRO

PURPOSE To automate repetitive editing tasks. A *macro* consists of recorded keystrokes and commands that perform a task. Macros are ideal for editing tasks that you perform regularly. They save time and reduce the chance of errors, since to perform the task, you simply replay the macro.

TO RECORD A MACRO

1. Select Macro ➤ Record or press Ctrl+F10. The Record Macro dialog box is displayed.

2. In the Filename text box enter a one- to eight-character name for the macro.

3. In the Descriptive Name text box enter a brief description of the macro's purpose. This step is optional but highly advisable. You can also enter a more lengthy description of the macro in the Abstract text box.

4. Select Record or press ↵. You are returned to the editing screen.

5. Enter the text and commands that you want in the macro. While a macro is recording, the status bar displays "Recording Macro." In addition the mouse pointer displays as a circle with a diagonal line through it when it's in the text area of the screen. This is to remind you that while recording a macro, you cannot use the mouse to move the insertion point or scroll (although you can use it to select commands). You must use the keyboard to move the insertion point while recording a macro.

6. When you have completed the desired actions, select Macro ➤ Stop or press Ctrl+Shift+F10.

TO REPLAY A MACRO

1. Select Macro ➤ Play or press Alt+F10. The Play Macro dialog box is displayed.

2. Type the macro name into the Filename text box, or select it from the Files list box.

3. Press ↵ or select Play.

NOTES A macro can contain text that becomes part of your document, Word-Perfect for Windows commands (such as those for formatting, printing, and saving a document), and special programming commands.

Margins

PURPOSE To control page margins. A margin is the distance between the edge of the page and your text. Each page has four margins, left, right, top, and bottom.

TO SET MARGINS

1. Move the insertion point to the location where you want the new margins to take effect.
2. Select Layout ➤ Margins or press Ctrl+F8. The Margins dialog box is displayed.
3. For each margin enter the desired value in the corresponding text box. You can also use the ↑ and ↓ keys to increase or decrease the margin setting by 0.01″.
4. Select OK or press ↵.

TO CHANGE MARGINS WITH THE RULER

1. Move the insertion point to the location where the new margins are to begin, or select the text to be affected by the new margins.
2. Point at the left or right margin symbol on the Ruler, and drag it to the desired location. As you move the symbol, a vertical dotted line shows in the document where the margin will be.
3. Release the mouse button.

NOTES The margins are measured in inches (or whatever measurement unit is in use) from the edge of the page. The default setting for all four margins is 1 inch.

See Also Auto Code Placement, Default Initial Codes, Indentation, Ruler, Units of Measure

MASTER DOCUMENTS

PURPOSE To manage large documents. You write your document in sections called subdocuments. You then create a master document that contains links to all the subdocuments. For example, a book could have each chapter in its own file, or subdocument.

TO CREATE A SUBDOCUMENT LINK

1. Move the insertion point to the location in the master document where you want the subdocument inserted.

2. Select Tools ➤ Master Document, and then choose Subdocument. The Include Subdocument dialog box is displayed.

3. Enter the name of the subdocument or select it from the list, and then select Include or press ↵.

4. A Subdocument Link code [Subdoc:] is inserted in the document and is represented on the screen as a comment.

TO EXPAND A MASTER DOCUMENT

When you expand a master document, the linked subdocuments are retrieved into the master document. To expand, select Tools ➤ Master Document ➤ Expand Master. In an expanded master document the start and end of each subdocument's text are marked by comments.

TO CONDENSE A MASTER DOCUMENT

When you condense a master document, subdocuments are removed (but the links remain).

1. Select Tools ➤ Master Document ➤ Condense Master.

2. In the dialog box select Yes if you want subdocument changes saved, or select No if you don't want subdocument changes saved.

NOTES A master document may contain only formatting and subdocument codes, or it may contain its own text as well.

You can edit subdocument contents while a master document is expanded. When you later condense the master document, you have the option of saving or discarding changes you made to subdocuments.

You can use addenda such as tables of contents and lists in a master document. Simply include the required codes in the subdocuments as you would in a normal document. After expanding the master document, be sure to select Tools ➤ Generate to be sure all addenda are up to date.

See Also   Index, Link, Lists, Table of Contents

MERGE OPERATIONS

PURPOSE   To combine information from two files to create a new document. The most common use of the Merge feature is to generate form letters using boilerplate text and a list of names and addresses. There are three components to a merge:

- ◆ The primary file contains the boilerplate text. This is the text that will be the same in each final merged document. The primary file also contains merge codes that instruct WordPerfect for Windows about how the merge is to proceed.

- ◆ The secondary file contains the information, such as names and addresses, that is to be inserted into the primary file. Information in a secondary file is organized into records, and each record contains one or more fields. A field has a name, and contains one piece of information, such as a name, city, or zip code. A record is a group of fields containing all the information for one individual.

- ◆ The merged document is the result of a merge operation. It consists of multiple copies of the primary file document, each including the information from one record in the secondary file.

TO CREATE A SECONDARY MERGE FILE

1. Decide what information the secondary file should contain, and how it should be broken down into fields.

2. Start with a new, empty document.

3. Type in the data for the first field of the first record. Do not press ↵ unless you want the field split over two or more lines.

4. Select Tools ➤ Merge or press Ctrl+F12, and then select End Field. You can also press the shortcut key Alt+↵. An {END FIELD} code and a hard return are inserted at the end of the line.

5. Repeat steps 3 and 4 for each field in the record. Fields are numbered sequentially, and the status line displays the number of the field you are currently entering.

6. After entering the last field of the record, select Tools ➤ Merge or press Ctrl+F12, and then select End Record. You can also press the shortcut key Alt+Shift+↵. An {END RECORD} code is inserted.

7. Repeat steps 3 through 6 for all records in the secondary file. Do not insert an {END RECORD} code at the end of the last record.

8. Save the file to disk as usual.

TO CREATE A PRIMARY MERGE FILE

1. Start with a new, empty document. Enter the boilerplate text as needed.

2. Move the insertion point to the location where you want a field from the secondary file inserted.

3. Select Tools ➤ Merge or press Ctrl+F12, and then select Field.

4. In the dialog box enter the number of the desired field or its name (if you named the fields in the secondary file—see the next section).

5. Select OK or press ↵.

6. Repeat steps 2–5 to insert additional fields in the primary file.

7. Save the file to disk as usual.

TO ASSIGN NAMES TO SECONDARY FILE FIELDS

1. Move the insertion point to the beginning of the secondary file.

2. Select Tools ➤ Merge or press Ctrl+F12, and then select Merge Codes.

3. In the dialog box list scroll until the {FIELD NAMES} code is highlighted, and then select Insert or press ↵. Another dialog box is displayed.

4. Type the name you want to use for the first field in each secondary file record, and then select Add.

5. Select Field Name to enter another name to be used for the next field.

6. Repeat steps 4 and 5 to assign names to all fields in the secondary file. Names are assigned to fields in order.

7. Select OK, and then select Close. The {FIELD NAMES} code is inserted into the document.

TO PERFORM A MERGE

1. Start with a new, empty document.

2. Select Tools ➤ Merge or press Ctrl+F12, and then select Merge.

3. In the dialog box enter the names of the primary and secondary files.

4. Select OK or press ⏎. The merge is performed and the resulting document is created in the window, with the insertion point at the end.

NOTES Merging is a complex topic, and can provide very powerful document handling capabilities. The above is only a brief introduction; you should refer to the WordPerfect for Windows documentation for additional information.

MOVING TEXT

PURPOSE To move text and/or codes from one location to another.

TO MOVE TEXT AND/OR CODES

1. Select the text and/or codes to be moved.

2. Select Edit ➤ Cut, press Shift+Del, or click the Cut button on the Button Bar.

3. Move the insertion point to the destination location.

4. Select Edit ➤ Paste, press Shift+Ins, or click the Paste button on the Button Bar.

See Also Copying Text, Selecting Text

OPENING A FILE

PURPOSE To read a document from disk into a new window for editing, printing, and so on.

TO OPEN A FILE

1. Select File ➤ Open, press F4, or click the Open button on the Button Bar.
2. If you know the filename, you can type it into the Filename text box.
3. Select the desired file from the Files list box. Use the Directories list box to change to another drive and/or directory, if needed.
4. Press ↵ or select Open.

See Also Retrieving a File

OUTLINE

PURPOSE To create outlines in a number of different styles. When you create or edit an outline, the headings are automatically numbered.

TO CREATE AN OUTLINE

1. Move the insertion point to the desired location.
2. Select Tools ➤ Outline ➤ Outline On.
3. Press ↵ to insert a first level paragraph number. Then type in the text for that outline entry.
4. Press ↵ to insert another entry at the same level as the previous one. If desired, press Tab to change to the next lower level or Shift+Tab to change to the next higher level.
5. Type in the text for the new outline entry.
6. Repeat steps 4 and 5 until the outline is complete.
7. Select Tools ➤ Outline ➤ Outline Off.

TO DEFINE OUTLINE NUMBERING STYLE

WordPerfect has a default outline numbering style that will be used if you do not redefine it. When you change the outline definition, the new definition affects all outlines from the insertion point onward.

1. Select Tools ➤ Outline ➤ Define or press Alt+Shift+F5. The Define Paragraph Numbering dialog box is displayed.

2. Open the Predefined Formats pop-up list and select a format. Select User Defined to create your own numbering format.

3. The box to the right displays the current numbering style associated with each level. Select the level whose style you want to change.

4. Open the Style pop-up list and select the desired style. The display box reflects the newly selected style.

5. Repeat steps 3 and 4 until all level styles are defined as you want them.

6. Select OK or press ↵.

TO SELECT AN OUTLINE STYLE

Outline style is different from outline numbering style. An outline style is a collection of formatting commands that control the way each outline level appears. For example, level 1 could be in extra large boldface type, level 2 indented with large italic type, and so on. When you change an outline style, all outlines at that level automatically change to reflect the new style. WordPerfect for Windows comes with several predefined styles.

1. Select Tools ➤ Outline ➤ Define or press Alt+Shift+F5. The Define Paragraph Numbering dialog box is displayed. Under Current Outline Style the currently active style is listed (or *<none>* is displayed if no style is active).

2. Select Change. A list of available styles is displayed.

3. Use the mouse or keyboard to highlight the desired style, and then choose Select.

4. Select OK.

TO CREATE A NEW OUTLINE STYLE

1. Select Tools ➤ Outline ➤ Define or press Alt+Shift+F5. The Define Paragraph Numbering dialog box is displayed.

2. Select Change, and then select Create. The Edit Outline Style dialog box is displayed.

3. Enter a name and a description for the style.

4. Under Define Outline Style highlight the level whose style you are editing.

5. Select Open or Paired from the Style pop-up list to specify whether the style will be Open (the default) or Paired. The formatting for an Open style applies to that level and all lower levels in the outline (unless explicitly changed at a lower level). The formatting for a Paired style applies to that level only.

6. Select Edit. The Style Editor screen opens. This screen is like the Reveal Codes screen: you see the outline levels in the upper portion, and the associated codes in the lower portion. A [Par NUM:] code will already be inserted here, reflecting the outline level you are editing.

7. Enter the formatting codes and/or text that you want as part of the style for this level. When finished, select Close to return to the Edit Outline Style dialog box.

8. Repeat steps 4 through 7 to define the styles for additional levels. When all levels have been defined, select OK from the Edit Outline Style dialog box.

TO EDIT AN EXISTING OUTLINE STYLE

1. Select Tools ➤ Outline ➤ Define or press Alt+Shift+F5. The Define Paragraph Numbering dialog box is displayed.

2. Select Change. Highlight the style you want to edit, and then select Edit. The Edit Outline Style dialog box is displayed containing information about the selected style.

3. Highlight the level whose style you want to edit and select Edit.

4. The style editing screen is displayed. Make changes in the style as desired, and then select Close.

5. Repeat steps 3 and 4 as needed, and then select OK.

NOTES This section gives the basic information you need to create and define outlines. For additional details please see your WordPerfect for Windows documentation.

OVERSTRIKE

PURPOSE To create new characters by combining two or more keyboard characters.

TO CREATE AN OVERSTRIKE CHARACTER

1. Position the insertion point where you want the character.
2. Select Font ➤ Overstrike ➤ Create. The Create/Edit Overstrike dialog box is displayed.
3. Enter the characters you want combined. For example, to display a zero with a slash through it (Ø), you would enter 0/ (or /0, as order does not matter).
4. To use special characters in your overstrike, press Ctrl+W.
5. To control the appearance of the overstrike character, open the pop-up list by clicking the arrow at the end of the text box. A list of font attributes is displayed, from which you can select.
6. Select OK or press ⏎. The combination character is inserted in your document.

TO EDIT AN OVERSTRIKE CHARACTER

1. Position the insertion point after the overstrike character you want to edit but before the next overstrike character.
2. Select Font ➤ Overstrike ➤ Edit. The Create/Edit Overstrike dialog box is displayed, with the overstrike components displayed.
3. Make the desired changes, and then select OK or press ⏎.

NOTES Many characters that you might create with the overstrike feature are present in the WordPerfect Special Character sets.

See Also Special Characters

PAGE NUMBERING

TO DISPLAY AND PRINT PAGE NUMBERS

1. Move the insertion point to the first page where you want the page numbers to begin.

2. Select Layout ➤ Page or press Alt+F9, and then select Numbering. The Page Numbering dialog box is displayed.

3. Select the Position pop-up list. This list includes all the page number position options, with a checkmark next to the one currently in effect. From the list select the desired position option, or select No Page Numbering to turn off page numbers. The two miniature pages display how the selected position option will look.

4. To change the numbering style, open the Numbering Type pop-up list and select the desired style.

5. Select OK or press ↵.

TO SPECIFY A NEW PAGE NUMBER

1. Move the insertion point to the page where the new numbering is to start.

2. Select Layout ➤ Page or press Alt+F9, and then select Numbering. The Page Numbering dialog box is displayed.

3. In the New Page Number text box enter the new page number, and then press ↵ or select OK.

TO SUPPRESS PAGE NUMBERS FOR ONE PAGE

1. Move the insertion point to the page where you do not want a page number.

2. Select Layout ➤ Page or press Alt+F9, and then select Suppress.

3. Select the Page Numbers option, and then select OK or press ↵.

NOTES Page numbers are normally printed as numerals only. To include accompanying text (for example, Page 1, Page 2), enter the desired text in the Accompanying Text box in the Page Numbering dialog box. The page number itself is represented by ^B in this box.

See Also Default Initial Codes, Headers and Footers

PAPER SIZE

PURPOSE To specify the size and orientation of printer paper. WordPerfect for Windows assumes that your document will be printed on standard $8\frac{1}{2} \times 11$ inch paper. You must inform the program if you will be using a different size.

TO CHANGE PAPER SIZE

1. Move the insertion point to the start of the document, or insert a hard page break at the page where the new paper type is to take effect.
2. Select Layout ➤ Page or press Alt+F9.
3. Select Paper Size. The Paper Size dialog box is displayed, with the current paper type is highlighted in the list.
4. Use the mouse and scroll bar, or the PgUp, PgDn, ↑, and ↓ keys to scroll in the list of paper types. Move the highlight to the desired type.
5. Press ↵ or choose select.

NOTES Each paper type definition includes the specifics of that type, such as its size and orientation. WordPerfect for Windows has several predefined paper types that will meet most needs. The definition includes the following components:

- Paper size gives the dimensions of the paper. The horizontal measurement is always listed first. Thus, 8.5×11 paper is $8\frac{1}{2}$ inches wide and 11 inches long.

- Paper orientation specifies how the print is placed on the paper. The default portrait orientation prints lines of text parallel to the short edge of the paper. Landscape orientation prints lines of text parallel to the long edge of the paper. Landscape orientation is not available on some printers.

- Paper location specifies where the printer gets the paper. Contin (for continuous) refers to your printer's usual paper source: tractor-feed paper or sheet feeders for dot-matrix printers; the paper cassette for laser printers. Manual specifies that individual pages are hand-fed to the printer.

- Prompt is either Yes or No. If set to Yes, the program pauses before printing each page and prompts you to insert a sheet of paper. Use a prompt setting of Yes to manually feed single items, such as envelopes and letterhead stationery, to your printer.

When you change paper type, WordPerfect for Windows automatically changes formatting to take the new paper size into account. Margins, page centering, and other formats are all adjusted.

See Also Default Initial Codes

PASSWORD

PURPOSE To password-protect confidential documents from unauthorized access.

TO ASSIGN A PASSWORD TO A DOCUMENT

1. Open the document.

2. Select File ➤ Password.

3. Type in the password, and then select Set.

4. Type the password again for verification, and then select Set. The password will take effect when the document is saved.

TO CHANGE A DOCUMENT'S PASSWORD

1. Open the document using the original password.

2. Follow the steps to assign a password. The new password will take effect when the document is saved.

TO REMOVE PASSWORD PROTECTION

1. Open the document using the password.

2. Select File ➤ Password ➤ Remove.

3. Save the document to make the change effective.

NOTES You cannot open a password-protected document unless you know the password. Password protection extends to associated document files (for example, backup files).

Password protection does not prevent a file from being deleted.

PRINT PREVIEW

PURPOSE To let you see on screen exactly what the document will look like when printed.

TO PREVIEW THE CURRENT DOCUMENT

1. Move the insertion point to the page you want to preview.

2. Select File ➤ Print Preview or press Shift+F5.

TO CONTROL PRINT PREVIEW PAGE OPTIONS

Page Options control which page or pages you view on the Print Preview screen.

- ◆ Select Full Page to view a single full page.

- ◆ Select Facing Pages to view two facing pages. Even-numbered pages are displayed on the left and odd-numbered on the right.

- ◆ Select Prev Page or Next Page to view the previous or next page.

- ◆ Select Go To Page to view a specific page. When you select this command, a dialog box opens. Enter the desired page number and press ↵.

TO CONTROL THE PRINT PREVIEW VIEW

View commands control the way the preview is displayed. You use these commands to zoom in on a small part of the document or to view an entire page. Use low scale factors to view large areas with less detail, and use high scale factors to view small areas with more detail. View commands are available on the View menu and on the Button Bar.

- ◆ Select 100% to display the page at 100% scale.

- ◆ Select 200% to display the page at 200% scale.

- ◆ Select Zoom In to increase the scaling by 25%.

- ◆ Select Zoom Out to decrease the scaling by 25%.

- ◆ Select Zoom Area to zoom in on a selected area. When you select Zoom Area, crosshairs are displayed on the screen. Use the mouse to move the crosshairs to one corner of the area to be viewed. Press and hold the mouse button, drag the outline to the opposite corner, and release the button.

- ◆ Select Zoom to Full Width to display the entire width of the page.
- ◆ Select Reset to return the display to the default scale.

TO PAN TO DIFFERENT PORTIONS OF THE PAGE

You can pan only if the page is enlarged (that is, if both vertical and horizontal scroll bars are displayed at the edges of the preview page). You can pan in any direction by using the mouse and scroll bars, or by pressing the arrow keys. You can also pan directly to a specific location using the mouse alone:

1. Move the mouse pointer to any location on the page, and click. The pointer changes to a four-headed arrow, and a miniature version of the current page is displayed with a box outlining the portion of the page that is currently displayed.

2. Click anywhere on the miniature page to pan the display to be centered on that location. Or, drag the box to the desired location on the miniature page.

3. To cancel the panning action, click anywhere outside the miniature page or press Esc.

TO CLOSE THE PRINT PREVIEW SCREEN

- ◆ Select File ➤ Close, press Ctrl+F4, or click the Close button.

NOTES The editing screen is very similar to the final printed page, but it is not identical. For example, the editing screen cannot show a full page, nor does it display headers, footers, or page numbers. For an accurate picture of how your printout will look, you must use the preview feature.

The status bar at the bottom of the preview screen displays the scale, page number, and paper size of the page being viewed. The *scale* is the percent size of the screen image relative to the final printed page. For example, 100% is actual printed size and 50% is one-half of printed size.

PRINTING FILES

TO PRINT THE ENTIRE DOCUMENT

1. Select File ➤ Print, press F5, or click the Print button on the Button Bar. The Print dialog box is displayed.

2. Select Print or press ↵.

TO PRINT THE CURRENT PAGE

1. Select File ➤ Print, press F5, or click the Print button on the Button Bar. The Print dialog box is displayed.

2. In the Options section of the dialog box select Current Page.

3. Select Print or press ↵.

TO PRINT A RANGE OF PAGES

1. Select File ➤ Print, press F5, or click the Print button on the Button Bar. The Print dialog box is displayed.

2. In the Options section of the dialog box select Multiple Pages.

3. Select Print or press ↵. The Multiple Pages dialog box is displayed.

4. In the Range text box enter the range of pages to print.

5. Select Print or press ↵.

TO PRINT SELECTED TEXT

1. Select the text. It can be any length, from a few words to many pages.

2. Select File ➤ Print, press F5, or click the Print button on the Button Bar. The Print dialog box is displayed.

3. In the Options section of the dialog box, the Selected Text option should already be selected.

4. Select Print or press ↵.

NOTES During printing, WordPerfect for Windows displays a status box that informs you of its progress in preparing the document for printing. When the status box is removed, you can return to working as the printing takes place. You can continue to edit the document, but changes made now will not be present in the printout.

When entering a page range in the Multiple Pages dialog box, use the formats shown in these examples:

1–5	Print pages 1 through 5
1, 3, 5	Print pages 1, 3, and 5
1–5,10–15	Print pages 1 through 5 and 10 through 15
1–5,7	Print pages 1 through 5 and page 7

If you have used the New Page Number command to reset page numbering in your document, WordPerfect for Windows treats the document as though it consists of a number of sections. Section 1 is from the beginning of the document up to the first New Page Number code, section 2 is from the first to the second New Page Number code, and so on. When specifying pages to print, enter the section number first followed by a colon and the page(s). If you do not specify a section, the first section is assumed:

2:1–5	Print pages 1 through 5 in section 2
1–5,2:7	Print pages 1 through 5 in section 1 and page 7 in section 2

When you print a selected section of text, it is printed in its "proper" position on the page. For example, if you select a single paragraph near the middle of a page, it is printed in the middle of an otherwise blank page.

See Also Page Numbering, Print Preview

REDLINE/STRIKEOUT

PURPOSE To display text with the redline or strikeout attributes. Strikeout places a horizontal line through text. Redline is displayed in red (or in reverse video on monochrome monitors), and can be printed in different ways (see below).

TO ADD REDLINE OR STRIKEOUT AS YOU TYPE

1. Select Font ➤ Redline or Font ➤ Strikeout to begin redline or strikeout.
2. Type the text.
3. Select Font ➤ Redline or Font ➤ Strikeout again to end redline or strikeout.

TO ADD REDLINE OR STRIKEOUT TO EXISTING TEXT

1. Select the text.
2. Select Font ➤ Redline or Font ➤ Strikeout.

TO CONTROL THE WAY REDLINE IS PRINTED

1. To change redline printing for the current document, select Layout ➤ Document ➤ Redline Method. To change redline printing for all new documents, select File ➤ Preferences.
2. In the dialog box, select the desired redline method:

   ◆ If you select Printer Dependent, the appearance of redline text will depend on your printer. On most laser printers, redline text has a shaded background.

   ◆ If you select Mark Left Margin, redline text is marked with a character in the left margin.

- If you select Mark Alternating Margins, redline text is marked with a character in the left margin on even-numbered pages and in the right margin on odd-numbered pages.

3. If you select one of the margin marking methods, you can enter the marking character in the Redline Character box. The default is a vertical line. To specify a special character, press Ctrl+W.

NOTES Redline attribute is commonly used to mark text that has or might be added to a document, and Strikeout is used for text that has been or might be deleted.

See Also Compare Documents

REPLACING TEXT

See Searching for and Replacing Text

RETRIEVING A FILE

PURPOSE To read a document from disk into the current window. If the window already contains a document, the retrieved file is added to it.

TO RETRIEVE A FILE

1. Move the insertion point to the location where you want the file placed.

2. Select File ➤ Retrieve.

3. If you know the filename, you can type it into the Filename text box.

4. Select the desired file from the Files list box. Use the Directories list box to change to another drive and/or directory, if needed.

5. Press ↵ or select Retrieve.

NOTES The contents of the retrieved file are added to the current document at the insertion point.

See Also Opening a File

REVEAL CODES

PURPOSE To view document formatting codes.

TO TURN REVEAL CODES DISPLAY ON OR OFF

- ◆ Select View ➤ Reveal Codes or press Alt+F3.

TO CHANGE THE SIZE OF THE REVEAL CODES WINDOW

1. Move the mouse pointer to the horizontal line that separates the Reveal Codes display from the regular editing screen. The pointer will change to a double-headed arrow.

2. Drag the line to the desired position, and then release the mouse button.

NOTES The Reveal Codes window has a cursor that corresponds to the position of the insertion point in the document. You can delete text and codes in the Reveal Codes window using the same methods used for text in the document.

RULER

PURPOSE To provide mouse shortcuts for certain formatting commands. The *ruler* can be displayed on the screen immediately beneath the Button Bar. The ruler and its

components are shown below. With the ruler, you can use the mouse to change margins, tab stops, font and font size, line spacing, and justification quickly. You can also apply styles and define tables and columns. For specific instructions, see the relevant entry.

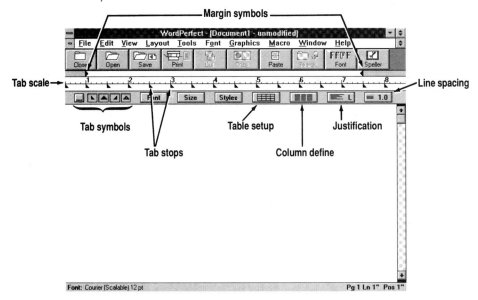

TO DISPLAY OR HIDE THE RULER

◆ Select View ➤ Ruler or press Alt+Shift+F3.

TO ASSIGN FONTS TO THE RULER

1. Select Font ➤ Font, press F9, or double-click the Font button on the ruler. The Font dialog box is displayed.

2. In the dialog box, select Assign to Ruler. The Ruler Fonts Menu dialog box is displayed.

3. This dialog box lists the available fonts (which depend on your printer) on the left. The fonts currently assigned to the Ruler are listed on the right.

4. To add a font to the Ruler, double-click it or highlight it and select Add.

5. To remove a font from the Ruler, double-click it or highlight it and select Clear.

6. When finished, select OK twice to return to the document.

TO MODIFY THE RULER SETTINGS

1. Select File ➤ Preferences ➤ Environment, or press Ctrl+Shift+F1, and then press **E**. The Environment Settings dialog box is displayed.

2. In the Ruler section you have the following options:

- ◆ Select Tabs Snap to Ruler Grid to have the ruler tab stops automatically snap to $\frac{1}{16}$-inch intervals.

- ◆ Select Show Ruler Guides if you want dotted indicator lines to appear in the document window when you are moving a tab stop or margin symbol on the ruler.

- ◆ Select Ruler Buttons on Top to have the button section of the ruler display at the top of the ruler rather than at the bottom.

- ◆ Select Automatic Ruler Display to have the ruler displayed in every new document window.

3. Select OK or press ↵.

NOTES In Draft display mode, the document text on screen may not accurately reflect the ruler's tab and margin settings.

See Also Columns, Font, Justification, Line Spacing, Margins, Styles, Tables, Tabs

SAVING A DOCUMENT

TO SAVE THE CURRENT DOCUMENT UNDER ITS EXISTING NAME

- Select File ➤ Save, press Shift+F3, or click the Save button on the Button Bar.

TO SAVE THE CURRENT DOCUMENT UNDER A NEW NAME

1. Select File ➤ Save As or press F3.
2. Enter the new filename in the dialog box.
3. Press ↵.

NOTES You should save a document regularly as you work on it to avoid the possibility of data loss.

See Also Opening a File, Retrieving a File

SEARCHING FOR AND REPLACING TEXT

TO SEARCH FOR TEXT

1. Select Edit ➤ Search, press F2, or click the Search button on the Button Bar. The Search dialog box is displayed.
2. Enter the search template in the Search For text box. To search for formatting codes, select Codes and select the desired codes from the Codes list.
3. If you want to search backward from the insertion point, select Direction, and then select Backward.
4. Select Search or press ↵ to begin the search.
5. If a match is found, the insertion point is positioned just after the matching text. If no match is found, a message is displayed in the status bar.

TO REPEAT A SEARCH

- ◆ To repeat the previous search forward from the insertion point, select Edit ➤ Search Next or press Shift+F2.

- ◆ To repeat the previous search backward from the insertion point, select Edit ➤ Search Previous or press Alt+F2.

TO SEARCH FOR AND REPLACE TEXT

1. Select Edit Replace or press Ctrl+F2. The Search and Replace dialog box is displayed.

2. Enter the target text in the Search For text box. To search for formatting codes, select Codes and select the desired codes from the Codes list.

3. Enter the replacement text in the Replace With text box. To simply delete occurrences of the target text, leave the Replace With text box blank.

4. If necessary, select Direction, and then select either Forward or Backward.

5. Select Search Next or press ↵ to start the process. WordPerfect for Windows finds and highlights the first occurrence of the target text. The dialog box remains displayed. You now have four choices:

   - ◆ Select Replace to replace the highlighted occurrence of the target text, and then find the next.

   - ◆ Select Replace All to replace all remaining occurrences of the target text.

   - ◆ Select Search Next to leave the highlighted occurrence of the target text unchanged, and then find the next.

   - ◆ Select Close to end the search and replace operation.

6. Repeat step 5 as many times as necessary. When the end of the document is reached, a message to that effect is displayed.

SELECTING TEXT

PURPOSE To specify the text to be affected by editing actions.

TO SELECT TEXT WITH THE MOUSE

1. Point at the start of the text.

2. Drag to the end of the text, and then release the mouse button.

TO SELECT TEXT WITH THE KEYBOARD

1. Move the insertion point to the start of the text.

2. Press and hold the Shift key.

3. Move the insertion point to the end of the text.

or

1. Move the insertion point to the start of the text.

2. Press and release the F8 key.

3. Move the insertion point to the end of the text.

TO SELECT TEXT USING SHORTCUTS

- ◆ To select a word, double-click anywhere in the word.

- ◆ To select an entire sentence, triple-click anywhere in the sentence.

- ◆ To select an entire paragraph, quadruple-click (four times!) anywhere in the paragraph.

TO DESELECT TEXT

- ◆ Press F8, *or*

- ◆ Click anywhere on the screen.

NOTES Selected text is highlighted on the screen.

SHORT MENUS

TO TURN SHORT MENU DISPLAY ON OR OFF

- ◆ Select View ➤ Short Menus.

NOTES With short menu display, on menus contain only the most frequently needed commands.

SORT

PURPOSE To sort the lines or paragraphs in a document, or rows in a table.

TO SORT ALL OR PART OF A DOCUMENT

1. If you do not want to sort the entire document, select the text to be sorted. To sort table rows, place the insertion point in the table.
2. Select Tools ➤ Sort or press Ctrl+Shift+F12. The Sort dialog box is displayed.
3. Under Record Type select the type of item being sorted.
4. Under Sort Order select Ascending or Descending sort.
5. By default, the sort is based on the first word in each item. To use additional or different sort keys, add/modify Key Definitions (as explained below).
6. Select OK or press ↵.

TO ADD OR MODIFY KEY DEFINITIONS

1. Be sure the proper option is selected under Record Type.
2. To add a key, select Insert Key.
3. The column headings in the Key Definition section indicate the criteria that the sort can be based on. The criteria available depend on the type of sort selected under Record Type.

4. The active key is marked by the > symbol. In the text boxes under Key Definitions enter numbers that specify each item's key position. For example, in a Line sort you might want the first word in each line to be key 1 and the second word in each line to be key 2. You would enter 1 in the Word column for key 1, and 2 in the Word column for key 2.

5. The default Type is Alpha (for alphanumeric). If desired, open the Type pop-up box and select Numeric. Use Numeric to sort numbers.

6. To delete the active key, select Delete Key.

7. To perform the sort, press ↵ or select OK.

NOTES A line ends with a soft or hard return. A paragraph ends with two or more hard returns.

Use additional key definitions to control the sort when two or more items have the same first key. For example, to sort a list of names you would specify last name as key 1 and first name as key 2.

You cannot reverse a sort with Undo, so you should save a document before sorting it.

Formatting codes on a line will move with the line during a sort. Therefore you should, when possible, place codes at the start of the document or in the document's initial codes.

SPECIAL CHARACTERS

PURPOSE To insert special characters and symbols in a document.

TO INSERT SPECIAL CHARACTERS

1. Select Font ➤ WP Characters or press Ctrl+W. The WordPerfect Characters dialog box is displayed.

2. The Set pop-up box displays the name of the character set that is displayed in the window. To use another set, open the Set pop-up box and select the desired set.

S

3. In the character window, scroll if necessary to view all the available characters. To insert a specific character:

- Double-click the character. The dialog box remains open so you can click back and forth between the document and the dialog box to insert additional characters.

- Click the character once, and then select Insert (to insert the character and leave the dialog box open) or Insert and Close (to insert the character and close the dialog box).

- Press Alt+C to make the character list box active. Use the arrow keys to move the dotted outline to the desired character, and then select either Insert or Insert and Close.

4. If necessary, select Close to close the dialog box.

NOTES There are twelve different character sets available. To see all the characters in the sets, refer to Appendix O in the WordPerfect for Windows Reference manual.

SPELLER

PURPOSE To find spelling and other errors in a document.

TO CHECK SPELLING

1. Select Tools ➤ Speller, press Ctrl+F1, or click the Spell button on the Button Bar. The Speller dialog box is displayed.

2. Open the Check pop-up box and select the portion of the document to be checked. The default is Document, which means that the entire document will be checked.

3. Select Start. The Speller looks at each word in the document and compares it with the dictionary. When a word is found that is not in the dictionary, the speller highlights the word in the document and pauses. In the dialog box the Start command button changes to read Replace. In many cases the Speller will list suggested replacements for the word in the Suggestions box.

4. Examine the highlighted word. You have several options at this point:

- Select Add if the word is not misspelled and you want to add it to the dictionary.

- ◆ Select Skip Once to skip this instance of the word but flag future instances in the document.

- ◆ Select Skip Always to skip this and all future instances of the word in the document.

- ◆ Select Replace to replace the highlighted word in the document with the highlighted word in the Suggestions list box. To highlight a different word in the Suggestions list, click the word or use the arrow keys.

- ◆ To edit the highlighted word in the document, click it and edit as usual. The Replace button in the dialog box will change to Resume. When you're finished editing the word, select Resume to continue with the spelling check.

- ◆ Select Close to terminate the spell check operation.

5. The Speller will also flag words that contain numbers, duplicate words, and words with irregular capitalization. To disable these features, display the Options menu in the Speller dialog box, and then select the desired feature.

6. When the spelling check is complete, a message to that effect is displayed. Select OK or press ↵.

See Also Thesaurus

STYLES

PURPOSE To automate text formatting and provide a consistent document appearance. A style is a collection of formatting codes saved together as a group. You can apply a style to an entire document or a portion of a document. Using styles for frequently used formats saves time and insures consistency. A style can include text as well as formatting codes.

TO CREATE A STYLE

1. Select Layout ➤ Styles or press Alt+F8, and then select Create. The Styles dialog box is displayed.

2. Select Create. The Style Properties dialog box is displayed.

3. Enter a name and description for the new style in the text boxes.

4. Open the Type pop-up list and select Open or Paired:

- An open style takes effect from the location at which it is inserted to the end of the document, or until it is changed by another style or code. You cannot turn off an open style.

- A paired style has two parts: Style On codes that take effect when the style is turned on, and Style Off codes that take effect when the style is turned off (see below for further information).

5. The Enter Key Inserts list offers three options that determine the action of the ⏎ key when you are using a paired style. These options have an effect only when you are creating a paired style:

- If you select Hard Return, pressing ⏎ while using a paired style has its normal effect, that is, inserts a [Hrt] code.

- If you select Style Off, pressing ⏎ while using a paired style turns the style off.

- If you select Style Off/On, pressing ⏎ while using a paired style turns the style off, and then back on again.

6. Select OK. The Style Editor window opens.

7. Enter the formatting commands and/or text to be part of the style. If you are creating a paired style, the Style Editor window includes a comment. Codes you place before the comment become part of the Style On codes; codes placed after the comment become part of the Style Off codes (see the Notes section for more information).

8. When the style is complete, select Close. You are returned to the Styles dialog box.

9. Select On to apply the style to the current document. Select Close to return to the document without applying the style.

TO APPLY AN OPEN STYLE TO TEXT

1. Move the insertion point to where you want the style to start.

2. Select Layout ➤ Styles or press Alt+F8. The Styles dialog box is displayed with a list of existing styles.

3. Select the style.

4. Select On.

TO APPLY A PAIRED STYLE TO TEXT

1. Move the insertion point to where you want the style to start.

2. Select Layout ➤ Styles or press Alt+F8. The Styles dialog box is displayed with a list of existing styles.

3. Select the style, and then select On.

4. Type in the text.

5. Select Layout ➤ Styles or press Alt+F8, and then select Off.

or

1. Select the text you want the style applied to.

2. Select Layout ➤ Styles or press Alt+F8. The Styles dialog box is displayed with a list of existing styles.

3. Select the style, and then select On.

TO EDIT A STYLE

1. Select Layout ➤ Styles or press Alt+F8. The Styles dialog box is displayed with a list of existing styles.

2. Select the style, and then select Edit. The Style Editor screen opens with the style's existing codes displayed.

3. Edit the codes as needed.

4. Select Close. Your changes will affect all instances of that style in the document.

NOTES When you apply a paired style, [Style On] and [Style Off] codes are inserted in the text. Following the location of the Style On code, the Style On formatting codes are applied to the text, up to the location of the Style Off code. After the Style Off code, the Style On formatting codes are turned off, and the Style Off formatting codes are applied.

When you apply an open style, a Style On code is inserted in the text. It affects the remainder of the document and cannot be explicitly turned off. Specific aspects of the style can be turned off or modified by another style or by individual formatting codes.

If the Ruler is displayed, you can click the Styles button and select a style from the pull-down menu.

See Also Ruler

S

SUBSCRIPT AND SUPERSCRIPT

PURPOSE To display text in a smaller font either raised (superscript) or lowered (subscript) with respect to the adjoining text.

TO CONVERT EXISTING TEXT TO SUBSCRIPT OR SUPERSCRIPT

1. Select the text.
2. Select Font, and then select Subscript or Superscript.

TO CREATE SUBSCRIPT OR SUPERSCRIPT AS YOU TYPE

1. Select Font, and then select Subscript or Superscript.
2. Type the text.
3. Select Font, and then select Subscript or Superscript again to return to normal text.

SUMMARY

See Document Summary

SUPERSCRIPT

See Subscript and Superscript

TABLE OF CONTENTS

PURPOSE To create a table of contents for a document automatically. The procedure involves three steps. First, you specify text in the document to be included in the table of contents. Next, you define the location and format of the table of contents. Finally you generate the table of contents.

TO SPECIFY TABLE OF CONTENTS ENTRIES

1. Select the word or phrase you want in the table of contents.
2. Select Tools ➤ Mark Text or press F12, and then select Table of Contents. The Mark Table of Contents dialog box is displayed.
3. Enter the level (1–5) that the text is to have in the table of contents.
4. Select OK or press ↵.

TO DEFINE THE TABLE OF CONTENTS

1. Move the insertion point to the location where you want the table of contents located. This will usually be at the beginning of the document.
2. Select Tools ➤ Define or press Shift+F12, and then select Table of Contents. The Define Table of Contents dialog box is displayed.
3. Enter the desired number of levels in the Number of Levels box.
4. For each level, open the corresponding pop-up box and select the desired numbering format for that level. The box on the right displays a sample of what the table of contents will look like with the currently selected options.
5. If you are using more than one level, select the Last Level in Wrapped Format option if you want the lowest level displayed wrapped flush instead of indented.
6. Select OK or press ↵.

TO GENERATE THE TABLE OF CONTENTS

1. Select Tools ➤ Generate or press Alt+F12, and then select Yes.

2. WordPerfect will generate the table of contents and all other addenda in the document (index and lists). A dialog box keeps you informed of progress.

NOTES If your table of contents definition specifies fewer levels than you used when marking text, the lower levels will be ignored when the table of contents is generated.

See Also Index, Lists

TABLES

PURPOSE To organize text or numbers in a row and column format. The general procedure is to first create the table, specifying how many rows and columns the table has. An empty table is then added to the document. Each cell in the table is labeled according to the row and column it is in. Rows are labeled alphabetically from left to right, and cells are labeled numerically from top to bottom. For example, the upper-left cell is A1.

To enter text in a table, move the insertion point to the desired cell and type the text. In a table the contents of each cell are restricted to that cell. You can edit text in a cell, and move and copy text between cells or between a cell and other parts of the document using the usual techniques.

You can format text in a table using the usual commands or using special commands found on the Table menu. You can also edit the table structure using commands on the Table menu: you can add or delete rows and columns, change column width, modify the lines displayed between cells, and so on.

TO MOVE BETWEEN CELLS IN A TABLE

1. To move to any cell, click in the cell.
2. If the insertion point is at the edge of a cell, the arrow keys will move to the next cell (or out of the table).
3. To move to the next or previous cell, press Tab or Shift+Tab. (To insert a Tab or Margin Release in a cell, press Ctrl+Tab or Ctrl+Shift+Tab.) Other movement keys are listed here:

    Home,Home   First cell in the row

End,End	Last cell in the row
Alt+←	One cell left
Alt+→	One cell right
Alt+↑	One cell up
Alt+↓	One cell down
Alt+Home	Top line in the cell
Alt+End	Bottom line in the cell

4. When the insertion point is in a table, select Edit ➤ Go To or press Ctrl+G, and then select a table destination from the Position pop-up list.

TO SELECT CELLS IN A TABLE

When you move the mouse pointer near the top border of a cell, it changes to an up-pointing arrow called the *vertical selection arrow*. When you move the mouse pointer near the left border of a cell, it changes to a left-pointing arrow called the *horizontal selection arrow*. You use the selection arrows to select cells, rows, and columns in a table:

- To select a single cell, position a vertical or horizontal selection arrow in the cell and click.

- To select a row, position a horizontal selection arrow in any cell in the row and double-click.

- To select a column, position a vertical selection arrow in any cell in the column and double-click.

- To select the entire table, position a vertical or horizontal selection arrow in any cell and triple-click.

You can select cells in a table using the keyboard as well. To select a single cell, move the insertion point to the first cell in the selection and press Shift+F8. To select multiple cells, first select one cell, and then extend the selection as follows:

| Shift+*arrow* | Extends the selection one cell in any direction. Can extend outside of the table. |
| Shift+Alt+*arrow* | Extends the selection one cell in any direction. Cannot extend outside of the table. |

Shift+Home	Extends the selection to the start of the current row.
Shift+End	Extends the selection to the end of the current row.
Shift+Ctrl+Home	Extends the selection to the start of the document.
Shift+Ctrl+End	Extends the selection to the end of the document.
Ctrl+↑ or ↓	Extends the selection to include the entire current column.
Ctrl+← or →	Extends the selection to include the entire current row.

TO INSERT ROWS AND COLUMNS IN A TABLE

1. Place the insertion point in a cell immediately to the right of or below where you want the new column(s) or row(s).

2. Select Layout ➤ Tables or press Ctrl+F9, and then select Insert.

3. In the dialog box select Rows or Columns, enter the number to insert, and then select OK or press ↵.

- ◆ You can insert a row at the insertion point position by pressing Alt+Ins, or below the insertion point position by pressing Alt+Shift+Ins.

- ◆ To add one or more columns at the right edge of a table, or one or more rows at the bottom of a table, select Layout ➤ Tables ➤ Options. Then, in the Table Size section of the dialog box change the Columns and/or Rows settings as desired, and select OK.

TO DELETE A SINGLE ROW OR COLUMN FROM A TABLE

1. Position the insertion point in any cell in the row or column.

2. Select Layout ➤ Tables or press Ctrl+F9, and then select Delete.

3. In the dialog box select Columns or Rows, and then press ↵ or select OK.

TO DELETE MULTIPLE ROWS OR COLUMNS FROM A TABLE

1. Select a group of cells that spans the rows or columns to be deleted.
2. Select Layout ➤ Tables or press Ctrl+F9, and then select Delete.
3. In the dialog box select Columns or Rows, and then press ↵ or select OK.

or

1. Move the insertion point to any cell in the first row or column to be deleted.
2. Select Layout ➤ Tables or press Ctrl+F9, and then select Delete.
3. In the dialog box select Columns or Rows, and then enter the number of columns or rows to delete.
4. Press ↵ or select OK.

TO DELETE TEXT AND/OR STRUCTURE IN A TABLE

- To delete some or all text within one cell, use the normal text deletion methods.
- To delete all text from one or more cells, select the cells and then press Del or Backspace. In the dialog box select Contents (Text Only), and then press ↵.
- To delete the table structure but retain the text, select the entire table, and then press Del or Backspace. In the dialog box select Table Structure (Leave Text), and then press ↵.
- To delete the entire table, both structure and text, select the entire table, and then press Del or Backspace. In the dialog box select Entire Table, and then press ↵.

TO MODIFY THE LINES BETWEEN CELLS IN A TABLE

1. To modify the lines around a single cell, move the insertion point to the cell. To modify the lines for a group of cells or the entire table, select the cells or the entire table.

2. Select Layout ➤ Tables or press Ctrl+F9, and then select Lines. The Table Lines dialog box is displayed.

3. The Left, Right, Top, and Bottom pop-up lists control the lines used for the four sides of each cell. For example, open the Left pop-up list and select the line style to be used for the left border of each cell in the selection.

4. The Inside pop-up list controls the line style used between cells within the current selection (valid for multi-cell selections only). For example, if you had selected the entire table, choose Dashed from the Inside pop-up list to display dashed lines between all cells in the table. This setting can override line styles specified in step 3.

5. The Outside pop-up list controls the line style used around the outside border of the selected cell or cells. For example, if you had selected the entire table, choose Thick from the Outside pop-up list to display thick lines around the outside of the table.

6. Once all line style selections have been made, select OK or press ↵.

TO JOIN TWO OR MORE CELLS INTO A SINGLE CELL

1. Select the cells to join.

2. Select Layout ➤ Tables or press Ctrl+F9, and then select Join.

3. If the cells you join contain text, WordPerfect for Windows inserts hard tab codes to format the text so it appears in the single cell similarly to how it appeared in the multiple cells before joining.

TO SPLIT A SINGLE CELL INTO MULTIPLE CELLS

1. Move the insertion point to the cell you want to split.

2. Select Layout ➤ Tables or press Ctrl+F9, and then select Split.

3. Select Columns (to split the cell vertically) or Rows (to split the cell horizontally), and then enter the number of cells to create.

4. Select OK or press ↵.

TO DEFINE A TABLE USING THE RULER

1. Move the insertion point to the desired table location.

2. Click the Ruler button that has a small table displayed on it. A grid of squares is displayed.

3. Drag the highlight to cover the number of squares vertically and horizontally corresponding to the number of rows and columns you want in the table.

4. Release the mouse button. The specified table is inserted in the document.

NOTES Tables are a powerful and complicated WordPerfect for Windows feature. This section covers only the most important table operations. Please see your program documentation for further information.

If you insert a new column in a table that is already at maximum width (that is, fills the space between the margins), the current column will be split into two columns. If the table is not at maximum width, the new column will be added without changing any existing columns.

See Also Columns, Ruler

TABS

PURPOSE To provide exact indentation within a document. WordPerfect for Windows comes with tabs preset every 0.5 inch. You can change the tab settings and the type of tabs used.

TO CHANGE TAB SETTINGS

1. Move the insertion point to the location where you want the new tab settings to take effect.

2. Select Layout ➤ Line or press Shift+F9, and then select Tab Set. The Tab Set dialog box is displayed.

3. The Position From option determines where tabs are measured from: the Left Edge of the paper or the Left Margin (as set with the Layout ➤ Margins command).

4. To clear all tabs, select Clear Tabs.

5. To clear one tab, highlight the tab in the Position list box and select Clear Tab.

6. To change the alignment of an existing tab, highlight the tab in the Position list, select the desired alignment under Tabs, and then select Set Tab.

7. To create a new tab stop, enter the desired tab position in the Position text box, select the desired alignment under Tabs, and then select Set Tab.

8. To make an existing or new tab a dot leader tab, select the Dot Leader option when creating or modifying the tab.

9. To return all tab stops to the default settings (left-aligned tab stop every 0.5 inch) select Default.

10. When finished, select OK or press ↵.

TO CREATE EVENLY SPACED TABS

1. Move the insertion point to the location where you want the new tab settings to take effect.

2. Select Layout ➤ Line or press Shift+F9, and then select Tab Set. The Tab Set dialog box is displayed.

3. Clear existing tabs by selecting Clear Tabs.

4. Select the Evenly Spaced option.

5. Select the type of tab alignment. The same alignment will be used for all tab stops.

6. Enter the position of the first tab stop in the Position box.

7. Enter the space between tab stops in the Repeat Every box.

8. Select OK or press ↵.

TO SET TABS WITH THE RULER

◆ To move an existing tab stop, drag it from its current position on the tab scale to the new location.

◆ To delete an existing tab stop, drag it off the page.

◆ To add a new tab stop, drag the desired tab symbol (from the set of tab symbols that are to the left of the Font button) to the desired position on the tab scale.

NOTES There are four types of tabs available. The type of a tab determines how text is aligned when you press Tab:

- ◆ Left aligned (the default) aligns text to the right of the tab; the left edge of the text is aligned with the tab stop.

- ◆ Right aligned aligns text to the left of the tab; the right edge of the text is aligned with the tab stop.

- ◆ Center aligns the text centered around the tab stop.

- ◆ Decimal aligned positions text so the decimal point is directly on the tab stop. You can specify characters other than the decimal point as the align character.

On the Ruler each type of tab stop is identified by a different symbol, as shown here:

left-aligned tab

center-aligned tab

right-aligned tab

decimal-aligned tab

Any tab type can be a *dot leader*. A dot leader tab displays a row of dots between the position where you press Tab and the next tab setting.

See Also Default Initial Codes, Indentation, Ruler

TEXT BOX EDITOR

PURPOSE To create or modify text in a Text Box, User Box, or Table Box (see the Graphics Boxes entry for further information).

TO CREATE OR EDIT TEXT IN A BOX

1. Select Graphics, and then select the type of box you want to edit (Text Box, Table Box, or User Box). Enter the number of the box to edit.

2. The Text Box Editor screen opens and displays the existing contents of the box, if any.

3. Enter text and formatting codes in the usual manner. You can use most formatting codes, create tables, define columns, and so on. You can also use File ➤ Retrieve to retrieve a file from disk into the Editor (as long as the file is less than one page). Any commands that are not available in the Text Box Editor will be grayed on the menus.

4. To rotate text in the box by 90, 180, or 270 degrees, select Rotate, and then choose the desired rotation angle.

5. To close the Text Box Editor and save your changes, select Close. To close without saving your changes, select Cancel.

NOTES Rotated text will be displayed on the Print Preview screen but not the normal document window. The ability to print rotated text depends on your printer.

To modify the position and size of the graphics box in the document, select Box Position.

See Also Graphics Boxes, Tables

THESAURUS

PURPOSE To find synonyms and antonyms for words.

TO USE THE THESAURUS

1. Position the insertion point within the word of interest.

2. Select Tools ➤ Thesaurus or press Alt+F1. The Thesaurus dialog box is displayed, with the selected word in the Word text box.

3. If the word is not found in the thesaurus, a message is displayed at the bottom of the dialog box. Otherwise, the first column displays alternatives for the word. The alternatives are displayed as follows (you may need to scroll to see the entire contents of the list box):

   ◆ At the top of the column is the *headword*, the word you selected in the document. Headwords are words that can be looked up in the thesaurus.

- Below the headword are listed *references*, words with meanings that are related to the headword. A reference may also be a headword (that is, it can be looked up), in which case it is marked with a bullet.

- References are divided into nouns (n), verbs (v), adjectives (a), and antonyms (ant). They may also be divided into subgroups if the headword has more than one meaning.

4. To replace the word in the document with one of the reference words, highlight the reference word, and then select Replace.

5. To look up another word in the thesaurus, type the new word into the Word text box and select Look Up.

6. You can also expand the lookup by double-clicking any reference word that is marked with a bullet. A hand pointer is placed next to the word, and the word becomes the headword in the next column, with alternatives displayed under it as explained above.

7. Repeat step 6 as many times as needed. Each time, a new group of alternatives will be created in its own column. Only three columns can be displayed at once. When more than three are open, scroll left and right by clicking the left and right arrow buttons.

NOTES Open the History menu to display a list of words you have looked up. If you select a word from the History menu, it becomes the new headword.

See Also Speller

UNDELETING TEXT

PURPOSE To restore text and/or codes you deleted from a document.

TO UNDELETE TEXT AND/OR CODES

1. Position the insertion point where you want the text/codes replaced. This does not have to be the location from where it was originally deleted.

2. Select Edit ➤ Undelete or press Alt+Shift+Backspace. The most recently deleted text is temporarily inserted in the document and highlighted, and a dialog box is displayed.

3. In the dialog box, select Restore to replace the highlighted text in the document. Select Next or Previous to view other blocks of deleted text. Select Cancel to close the dialog box without undeleting any text.

NOTES WordPerfect remembers your last three deletions. Undelete lets you restore text at the insertion point. This is different from Undo, which always restores deleted text at its original location.

See Also Undo

UNDERLINE

TO UNDERLINE EXISTING TEXT

1. Select the text.

2. Select Font ➤ Underline or press Ctrl+U.

TO UNDERLINE AS YOU TYPE

1. Select Font ➤ Underline or press Ctrl+U to begin underlining.

2. Type in the text.

3. Select Font ➤ Underline or press Ctrl+U again to end underlining.

NOTES Underlining can be combined with bold, italics, and other font attributes.

See Also Default Initial Codes, Double Underline, Selecting Text

UNDO

PURPOSE To reverse the most recent change to a document.

TO UNDO AN EDITING ACTION

- Select Edit ➤ Undo or press Alt+Backspace.

NOTES You can undo most actions, including typing or deleting text, changing format, and inserting graphics; however, you cannot undo certain actions such as sorting text, converting tabular columns to tables, merging text, and generating lists.

When used to restore deleted text, Undo replaces the text in its original location. This is different from Undelete, which restores the text at the insertion point.

You cannot undo actions that do not change the document, such as scrolling or moving the insertion point.

See Also Undelete

UNITS OF MEASURE

PURPOSE To specify the units to be used for display and entry of on-page measurements.

TO SPECIFY UNITS OF MEASURE

1. Select File ➤ Preferences ➤ Display. The Display Settings dialog box is displayed.

2. In the Units of Measure section there are two pop-up lists:

- Display and Entry of Numbers controls the units used in dialog box display and entry (for example, when setting margins).

- Status Bar Display controls the units used in the status bar display.

3. Select a unit of measure, and then select OK.

NOTES You can select from five units of measure:

- Select i or ″ for inches (displayed as 2i or 2″).

- Select c for centimeters.

- Select p for points (1 point = $\frac{1}{72}$ inch).

- Select w for 1200ths of an inch.

You can enter a setting in any unit by including the corresponding letter after the number. For example, if measurements are set to inches but you want to specify a margin of two centimeters, enter 2c in the Margins dialog box. The program automatically converts it to inches.

WIDOW/ORPHAN PROTECTION

PURPOSE To prevent the last line of a paragraph from printing by itself at the top of a page (a *widow*), or the first line of a paragraph from printing by itself at the bottom of a page (an *orphan*).

TO PREVENT WIDOWS AND ORPHANS

1. Move the insertion point to the document location where you want protection to start.

2. Select Layout ➤ Page or press Alt+F9.

3. Select Widow/Orphan. Protection extends to the end of the document or to the location where you turn protection off by selecting Layout ➤ Page ➤ Widow/Orphan again.

NOTES When widow/orphan protection is on, the next-to-last line of a paragraph is moved to the next page to join a widow, and an orphan is moved to the next page to print with the rest of the paragraph.

See Also Block Protect, Conditional End of Page, Default Initial Codes

WORD COUNT

PURPOSE To count the number of words in a document.

TO OBTAIN A WORD COUNT

1. To count words in a block of text, select the text.

2. Select Tools ➤ Word Count.

3. WordPerfect for Windows counts the words in the text selection or document, and displays the total.

APPENDIX

*I*NSTALLING WORDPERFECT FOR WINDOWS

INSTRUCTIONS FOR INSTALLATION

Before you can use WordPerfect for Windows, you must install it on your system. The process is not difficult, as an automated INSTALL program does most of the work for you. You need only to insert a few disks and answer some questions. Before you start, you need to know the make and model of the printer you will be using. You should also make backup copies of the WordPerfect for Windows disks. Store the original diskettes in a safe place, and use the backups for installation.

1. If you are running Windows, exit to DOS. The Install program must be run from the DOS prompt.

2. Log on to the hard disk on which you want to install WordPerfect for Windows.

3. Insert the Install diskette in drive A: or B:, and then enter **A:INSTALL** (or **B:INSTALL**).

4. The Install program will start and you will be offered a list of installation choices. Most first-time installers should select Basic, which will install the standard WordPerfect files to default locations. Select Custom only if you have reason to believe that the standard installation is not suitable, and you are familiar with the program files and your disk directory structure. For example, you might want to install the program in a different directory or to install only a subset of the program files. The remainder of these instructions assume that you have chosen Basic Installation.

5. The rest of the installation process requires you to answer a few on-screen questions and swap diskettes when requested. Information in the following steps will help you answer the questions.

6. WordPerfect for Windows comes with several video drivers, or monitor files, that allow the program to interact with different kinds of video hardware. The Install program will detect the type of monitor installed in your system. You will be asked whether to install all monitor files instead of only the file for the monitor in your system. Unless you expect to be using different types of video hardware, answer No.

7. You can choose between two keyboard layouts: the CUA (Common User Access) layout (the Windows standard) or the layout used by WordPerfect 5.1 for DOS. Even if you are very familiar with the DOS WordPerfect keyboard commands, I suggest that you select the CUA layout. You need to learn it sometime, and the sooner you start the easier it will be! Also, both the WordPerfect for Windows manual and this book assume the CUA layout. You can always switch between keyboard layouts while running the program: select File ➤ Preferences ➤ Keyboard ➤ Select, and then choose the desired layout from the list.

8. During installation you must select one or more printer drivers. You can use the Windows drivers or the WordPerfect drivers. I suggest you choose the latter, as the WordPerfect drivers print faster. You can always switch to a Windows driver if necessary. When installing a WordPerfect printer driver, you will insert the Printer disk and select your printer from the list.

9. The final installation step asks if you want to view the READ.ME files. These files contain information about last-minute program changes that are not documented in the manual (or in this book!). It's a good idea to spend a few minutes reading this information.

10. When you are finished with installation, you will be returned to the DOS prompt. You can start Windows, and then turn to Lesson 1.

INDEX

A

abstracts
  of documents, 122
  of macro, 70
active document windows, 92, 94
Alpha sort type, 188
anchors, for graphic boxes, 138
annotations, for help, 144
appending text, 103
auto code placement, 103
automatic backup, 104

B

^B (page number code), 141
Backspace key, 10, 22, 120
backup copies
  automatic, 104
  settings for, 81–82
Basic installation, 210
.BK! file name extension, 81, 104
black and white graphic image, 127
block protect, 105
  parallel columns with, 112
boilerplate text, 165
bold type, 35, 105
Bookmark ➤ Define, 145
border, for graphic boxes, 137
bottom margin, 53–54
Button Bar, 11, 106–107
  adding macros to, 106
  Close button, 109
  Copy button, 23, 97, 115
  Cut button, 23, 97, 167
  for Figure Editor, 128
  Font button, 130

Open button, 16, 92
Paste button, 98, 115, 167
Print button, 64, 177
Save button, 184
Search button, 24, 184
Spell button, 87

C

capitalization, spelling check of, 86, 87
captions, for graphic boxes, 136–137
cascade menus, 7
cascaded windows, 94
case conversions, 108
cells in tables, 195
  joining or splitting, 199
  selecting, 196–197
center-aligned tabs, 202
center-justification, 33–34, 154
centering text vertically, 55–56, 108–109
characters
  anchoring graphic boxes to, 138
  changing case of, 108
  overstrike to create, 171
  special, 85–86, 188–189
checkbox, 8, 10
clearing tabs, 200–201
clipboard. *See also* copying text; moving text
  adding text to, 103
Close button (Button Bar), 109
closing
  dialog boxes, 11
  document windows, 98–99
  documents, 109
codes. *See also* formatting codes
  for hyphenation, 146
Codes dialog box, 37, 38
columns, 110–112

Greek characters, 85
gutter space, between columns, 110

H

 CTRL +↵

hanging indent, 31, 149
hard page breaks, 52, 141
headers and footers, 45–49, 141–142
   discontinuing, 49, 142
   editing, 48
   page numbers in, 141
headword, 203
Help, 143–145
Help ➤ Index, 143
History menu (Thesaurus), 204
Home key, 10
horizontal selection arrow, 196
hyphenation, 145–147
hyphenation soft return, 147
hyphenation zone, 145

I

importing files, 148
indentation, 31–32, 148–149
   and margins, 53
index, 149–151
   manually specifying entries to,
      149–150
initial codes
   default, 78–79, 118–119
   document, 121
initial font, 42–43, 151
insertion, of table rows or columns, 197
insertion point, 5, 10, 12, 152
   Go To command to move, 134
   moving, 16–19
   moving in table, 195–196
   moving through columns, 111
   scrolling with mouse and, 18
installing WordPerfect for Windows,
      210–211
inverting graphic image, 127
italics, 35, 153

J

joining table cells, 199
jump terms in Help, 144
justification, 33–34, 154

K

key definitions, in sort feature, 187–188
keyboard, 9–10
   help for, 143
   layouts for, 154–155
   for menu selection, 6
   moving window with, 97
   resizing window with, 96
   selecting text with, 20, 186
   for table selection, 196–197
keyboard layouts, installing, 210
keystroke shortcuts. *See* shortcut keys

L

landscape orientation, 56, 173
language, 156
Layout ➤ Columns ➤ Define, 110
Layout ➤ Document
   ➤ Initial Codes, 121
   ➤ Initial Font, 43, 151
   ➤ Redline Method, 179
   ➤ Summary, 79, 122
Layout ➤ Endnote
   ➤ Create, 123
   ➤ Edit, 123
   ➤ New Number, 124
   ➤ Placement, 123
Layout ➤ Footnote
   ➤ Create, 131
   ➤ Edit, 131
   ➤ New Number, 132
   ➤ Options, 131
Layout ➤ Justification, 33, 154
Layout ➤ Line, 157
   ➤ Hyphenation, 145

M

SYBEX

FREE BROCHURE!

Complete this form today, and we'll send you a full-color brochure of Sybex bestsellers.

Please supply the name of the Sybex book purchased.

_____

How would you rate it?

_____ Excellent   _____ Very Good   _____ Average   _____ Poor

Why did you select this particular book?

_____ Recommended to me by a friend

_____ Recommended to me by store personnel

_____ Saw an advertisement in _____

_____ Author's reputation

_____ Saw in Sybex catalog

_____ Required textbook

_____ Sybex reputation

_____ Read book review in _____

_____ In-store display

_____ Other _____

Where did you buy it?

_____ Bookstore

_____ Computer Store or Software Store

_____ Catalog (name: _____)

_____ Direct from Sybex

_____ Other: _____

Did you buy this book with your personal funds?

_____ Yes   _____ No

About how many computer books do you buy each year?

_____ 1-3   _____ 3-5   _____ 5-7   _____ 7-9   _____ 10+

About how many Sybex books do you own?

_____ 1-3   _____ 3-5   _____ 5-7   _____ 7-9   _____ 10+

Please indicate your level of experience with the software covered in this book:

_____ Beginner   _____ Intermediate   _____ Advanced

Which types of software packages do you use regularly?

_____ Accounting	_____ Databases	_____ Networks
_____ Amiga	_____ Desktop Publishing	_____ Operating Systems
_____ Apple/Mac	_____ File Utilities	_____ Spreadsheets
_____ CAD	_____ Money Management	_____ Word Processing
_____ Communications	_____ Languages	_____ Other _____
		(please specify)

Which of the following best describes your job title?

_____ Administrative/Secretarial _____ President/CEO

_____ Director _____ Manager/Supervisor

_____ Engineer/Technician _____ Other _____
                                              (please specify)

Comments on the weaknesses/strengths of this book: _____

_____

_____

_____

_____

Name _____

Street _____

City/State/Zip _____

Phone _____

PLEASE FOLD, SEAL, AND MAIL TO SYBEX

SYBEX, INC.
Department M
2021 CHALLENGER DR.
ALAMEDA, CALIFORNIA USA
94501

SYBEX

SEAL